White Pine tree overlooking historic Lac des Chats formerly The Hill residence of the first Daniel McLachlin, built in 1853. The White Pine was the unanimous choice of the Ontario Tree Council, representing 30 tree and forestry organizations, as Ontario's official tree. Ontario becomes the first Canadian province to adopt an official tree.

A fitting commemoration of the Bi-Centennial of Ontario.

The Arnprior Story

1823-1984

BY LEO LAVOIE

A HISTORY OF ARNPRIOR

Published by

H. Brittle Printing Limited

ON THE OCCASION OF

THE BI-CENTENNIAL OF THE PROVINCE OF ONTARIO

Copyright © 1984 Leo Lavoie
Registration No. 330646

All rights reserved by author

Canadian Cataloguing in Publication Data

Lavoie, Leo, 1913-
    The Arnprior Story

Includes Index

ISBN 0-9691899-1-5

1. Arnprior (Ont.) — History
1. Title

FC3099.A74L39 1984a 971.3'81 C84-090206-9
F1059.5.A74L.39 1984b

First Printing Sponsored & Published by
Arnprior & District Historical Society, June 1984

Second Printing Published by
H. Brittle Printing Limited, Arnprior, Ontario, October 1984

Third Printing Published by
H. Brittle Printing Limited, Arnprior, Ontario, March 1985

Typesetting and Printing by H. Brittle Printing Limited
Arnprior, Ontario

Cover Photograph;
David A. Gillies Building, Library and Museum,
By Tom Hanson Photography ©.

TO ANNE
FOR HER TREMENDOUS PATIENCE
AND UNCEASING MORAL SUPPORT
THIS BOOK IS DEDICATED

AUTHOR'S NOTE

Most of us identify History with school days and the laborious task of memorizing in chronological order, events and dates connected primarily with Canadian, British and American history. The subject invariably is a dry one and, unless the student is actively interested in pursuing a teaching career in history, it is usually soon forgotten.

However, if we do not record the Past, we will not record the Future and we shall remain only in the vacuum of the Present. The history of Arnprior has swung on the hinges of the lumbering era to the present highly diversified industrial age. I have long hoped to attempt an in-depth story of the rise and decline of one of the largest producers of sawn lumber on the North American Continent, McLachlin Brothers Limited, but realized it must, of necessity, not only encompass the founding industry but must recognize, in particular, a cosmopolitan people, those pioneers who hewed this settlement from the wilderness.

This is not a legend, not fictitious, but rather a true story coming down from the past. It is a history of Arnprior, its people and its industry.

I am deeply indebted to a great many people who have contributed in making this project possible and I have scrupulously acknowledged their contributions within this book. If any organization or individual has been overlooked, it has been inadvertent and my gratefulness applies to all. In gratitude and fairness, I must single out in particular, the Arnprior & District Historical Society and President Janet Clancy, also Kay Rogers, Chairperson of the grant structure committee, who secured the grants listed in this note without which this book could not have been published; Jean Macnamara Cunningham who made available to me all of her Uncle Charles Macnamara's documents and photographs; the Ontario Archives and Public Archives; the Arnprior Museum Board and Curator Janet Carmichael; Anne Mulvihill for her permission to use the article by her late husband, Timothy C. Mulvihill, on the internal operation of the mills and yards; and my good friends Ernest B. Wolff, Eric Patterson (Pat) Hall; Edgar Harrington Burwash; the late Stewart Graham; and Tom Hanson who graciously provided many of the photographs.

To avoid cluttering up the text I have listed other credits on the last pages of this book.

GRANTS

Province of Ontario Bi-Centennial Committee and Town of Arnprior.

This project has received financial assistance from the Department of the Secretary of State of Canada to mark the Bi-Centennial of Ontario.

In appreciation of a Wintario Program Grant from the Ministry of Citizenship and Culture.

The second and third printings were produced without grants.

L.J.L.
Arnprior, 1985

CONTENTS

CONTENTS – Cont'd

Photo by Hanson

HISTORICAL SOCIETY EXECUTIVE
Standing left to right: Vice-President Edna Carey, Secretary Janet Carmichael, Treasurer Mabel Simpson.
Front left to right: Past President Ernest Wolff, President Janet Clancy.

FOREWORD

As a member of the McLachlin family it is an honor and a privilege to have been asked by Leo Lavoie, the author, to write the foreword to his book, *The Arnprior Story*.

The McLachlin family are indebted and grateful to Mr. Lavoie for his sensitive and factual depiction of the early days of the lumber industry and the McLachlin family and the growth of the town around the mills. A recent visit to the Western Highlands of Scotland was an excellent preparation for the writing of a foreword to this book dealing with Arnprior and its beginnings. A trip to the tiny hamlet of Arnprior near Stirling and a walk out on Inch Buie, the ancient burial ground of the Lairds of McNab on an island set in the rushing white waters of the Dochart River at Killen, made me feel very close to those early settlers who came to our Arnprior. A visit to the castle of the McLachlans on Loch Fyne in Argyle and the opportunity of meeting the present chief of the Clan, Dame Marjorie McLachlan, was an unforgettable experience.

The family name is carried on with the present Daniel McLachlin who is living in Calgary, and his young son, Hugh Frederick; they are son and grandson of Hugh Frederick McLachlin presently living in Burlington, Ontario.

Norma C. Hall.

NORMA HALL

MESSAGE FROM THE MAYOR

The Citizens of Arnprior are indebted to the Arnprior & District Historical Society, Author Leo Lavoie and the Province of Ontario Bi-Centennial Committee for the dedication in preserving the History of Arnprior from 1823 to 1984, in this publication *"The Arnprior Story"*.

Arnprior is pleased to sponsor a portion of the cost, as one of their Bi-Centennial Programs recognizing two hundred years of this great Province of Ontario.

We trust this book will be circulated world wide and will become a focal point in our schools and libraries for all to refer to when questions arise of our history and our forefathers.

Many times history passes without documentation. We are proud people. This book depicts hard times, good times and above all our heritage which by it's publication preserves for all times Arnprior - its people from 1823 to 1984.

Our thanks to all those who have contributed to its works.

TOWN OF ARNPRIOR

Mayor T. E. Sullivan.

TOWN COUNCIL 1984

ARCHIBALD McNAB
LAST LAIRD OF THE CLAN McNAB

IT WAS A beautiful evening. The setting sun was casting shadows among the pines on the baronial estate of Dr. Hamilton Buchanan, the last Buchanan of the ancient house of Arnprior, Scotland. A horseman evidently in full flight, dismounted and tied the horse at a point near the park. This was Archibald McNab, at age 42, the Last Laird of the Clan McNab.

The affairs of McNab were thought to be involved beyond extrication; his estate was mortgaged to the Earl of Breadalbane and officers of the law were on his track. By a private gate he entered the halls of Leney, the palatial mansion of his cousin Dr. Buchanan where he hoped to take refuge from his pursuers. With the further aid of friends, one of whom was Peter McIntyre who died in Calabogie in 1868, McNab set out for Dundee and from there he sailed for London, and on to Quebec where he hoped to found a settlement, retrieve his lost fortunes and eventually return to his native Scotland.

Upon arrival in Quebec, McNab went on to Montreal and then journeyed to Glengarry where he met Bishop Mac-Donnell who told him of the Ottawa. Chief McNab commenced negotiations with the government of Upper Canada offering to found a Highland settlement like that which existed on the banks of the St. Lawrence. The government informed him that a township had been recently surveyed adjoining Fitzroy, comprised of 81,000 acres. It had not yet been named and if he undertook the settlement McNab could name it after himself.

He agreed to the terms and promptly called the township McNab, without ever seeing the area and without any knowledge of its facilities. He then wrote friends in Scotland asking them to send twenty families to settle in the new township of McNab. On April 19, 1825, the McNab settlers, some 84 men, women and children embarked at Greenock for America, arriving in Montreal on May 27, where they were met by Chief McNab. Their luggage was transported by ox cart to Hawkesbury by the forwarding company operated by the father of Arnprior's first Daniel McLachlin. The settlers with their families made the journey on foot. They then boarded the steamboat "Union" and arrived in Hull two days later. From Hull upwards the settlers travelled by steamer, enduring many hardships,

finally reaching the Chats, where they again made their way through the bush, following a pathway and guided by a blaze. The journey from Montreal to McNab took 28 days.

They arrived at the foot of John Street at a point then known, and still recognized, as the "wharf", where they pitched their tents. McNab had erected a log mansion on the summit of the adjacent hill, later the location of the palatial residence of Daniel McLachlin, and called it Kennell Lodge after his Scottish estate. McNab accommodated as many as possible in Kennell Lodge, while the remainder of the settlers occupied the camps until all luggage was brought up.

The Chief then called the group together and informed them that the government had given him the township as a grant because he was a Highland Chief, a statement altogether untrue. The settlers had every confidence in the Chief and set out to select their lands; some went up the Madawaska River; others selected lands in the Flat Rapid section; others went to the borders of Horton; while the rest chose lands in the neighborhood of Arnprior and along the banks of the Dochart Creek, named after a river flowing through the Kennell estate in Scotland. They immediately commenced clearing the land, erecting their home shanties in the primeval forest.

Sitting in solemn state at Kennell Lodge, McNab proceeded to sign and seal the location tickets; a portion of the ticket reads as follows: "I hereby bind myself, my heirs and successors, to give you the said land free of any quit rent for three years from this date, as also to procure you a patent for the same at your expense, upon your having done the settlement duties and your granting me a mortgage upon said lands, that you will yearly thereafter pay to me, my heirs and successors forever one bushel of wheat or Indian corn, or oats of like value, for every cleared acre upon the said lot of land in name of quit rent for the same in the month of January in each year.

Signed and sealed, Archibald McNab."

This was not what the government had intended but the settlers were ignorant of the laws and had implicit confidence in their Chief. They bound themselves and their land to McNab, but a feeling of unrest soon became manifest. The story of discontent on the part of the settlers and persecution on the part of the Chief is a long one. McNab carried his Lairdship with a high hand, and he reduced the free-born Highlanders to the abject equivalent of serfs. The first open break came within two years. The Chief claimed the right to all the timber in the township and Alexander Miller, one of the settlers who was a school teacher and well educated, remonstrated with the Chief and said the settlers had a right to the timber and in defiance of the Laird's despotic commands, Miller sold all the timber on his land to John Brill formerly a lumberman of McNab. McNab was furious and vowed vengeance. He had influence with the government; Brill was compelled to pay the full amount of duty on the timber he cut and Miller was thrown into prison at the command of the Chief for an alleged debt of eighty pounds sterling. After six weeks in jail his kinsmen travelled sixty miles through the deep forest to offer bail and Miller was released for the time being. Miller eventually left the township and died in Beckwith in 1867, the first martyr to the Laird of McNab's despotism.

In the fall of 1831 Chief McNab met George and Andrew Buchanan in Montreal, spoke to them in glowing terms of the rapids at the mouth of the Madawaska River and persuaded them to settle in "his township". He made lavish promises of a mill site free, and timber for sawlogs for a trifling consideration. Further, he claimed them as distant relatives as descendants of the Buchanans of Arnprior, Scotland. The young men came to inspect the place and agreed to the Chief's terms and in compliment to McNab, as well as on account of their origin, they named the place Arnprior, and thus the Arnprior of Canada received its name.

The Buchanan brothers immediately commenced operations. The land was cleared, workshops of log were erected, a store and dwelling were built, a dam was thrown across the Madawaska, and a bridge spanned the river. A gristmill was erected on the small island near the bridge, and a sawmill constructed at the easterly end of the bridge. Early in 1833 the entire works were in operation and Arnprior became active for the first time.

In 1834 the Buchanans and Chief McNab had a serious confrontation which culminated in the Buchanans handing over their property to the firm of Gould, Simpson and Mittleberger. The persecution of the settlers by Chief McNab was becoming worse. By this time steamboats were plying regularly between Montreal and Fitzroy Harbour and the Buchanans were resolved to extend the service to the Chenaux Rapids and a steamer was in the course of construction when Andrew Buchanan fell ill and died. He was buried at a point near the corner of Daniel and Elgin Streets. The remains were later removed to the Arnprior cemetery. George continued the business after his brother's death but the dreams of the Buchanan brothers came to an end in 1836 the very year the steamboat "George Buchanan" was launched. The lumber business, so promising a few years ago, collapsed. Their holdings were taken over by Gould, Simpson and Mittleberger (as previously mentioned) later to be assigned to the Middletons of Liverpool.

George Buchanan left Arnprior to live on Chats Island, now known as Morris Island. He was accidentally killed in 1839 while engaged in freeing a timber "jam" in the rapids. In the meanwhile McNab proceeded with the clearing of a farm at White Lake and there erected Waba Lodge, the Chief's White Lake home.

Chief McNab's influence was steadily waning; every outrage was met by the settlers who were organized against him. At the Spring assizes at Perth in 1843 the Chief was arrested and brought to court as a public nuisance and a verdict of guilty was pronounced. It was the final culmination of the defeat of McNab's power. Soon after, he left McNab forever; he was forced to abandon a township where he might have lived happily and beloved and with the advantages he possessed he could have ended his days in wealth and influence. Chief McNab died on April 22, 1860 in the small village of Lanion, France.

At least one redeeming feature of his life is manifest, and that is that he caused to settle in McNab as loyal, persevering, thrifty and worthy a class of citizens as could be found anywhere.

THE MADAWASKA RIVER

THE MADAWASKA River plays an important role in this historical document and it is commonly conceded that the Indians gave this turbulent waterway its name. One version has this as meaning "Hidden River". Another, according to Armon Burwash, one-time executive member of the McLachlin firm, is said to have derived from "Mata" or "Meta", the fork or mouth of a river, and "Aushja" the sound of the rippling current at its mouth.

THE McLACHLIN DYNASTY — 1851-1929

A LONE STOCKILY-BUILT figure leaned against the bow-rail of the wood-burner steamer "Oregon" as it chugged its way up the choppy waters of Lac des Chats on a bright but windy day in mid-May 1851.

The face of the first Daniel McLachlin was one of contemplative study; his eyes riveted on the heavily timbered shoreline and the high bluff overlooking the majestic Ottawa River and the wooden wharf at the all but deserted hamlet of Arnprior, his destination.

As the "Oregon" edged against the dilapidated timbered dock a crew member jumped with the hawser line while another lowered the anchor on the starboard side of the vessel. McLachlin, with a light pack-sack strapped to his back, stepped to the dock and slowly made his way up the hill and along the dusty road, now John Street, in a southerly direction. The roar of rapids told him he was nearing the abandoned Buchanan holdings along the turbulent Madawaska River.

The awesome sight that greeted him must have left McLachlin with mixed feelings with regard to his timber expansion plans. Spring freshets had carried away a portion of the timbered bridge; the tiny gristmill situated on the small island near the eastern extremity of the bridge was a wreck; the sawmill was in ruins; all that remained were a few desolate and badly battered log buildings and a one-time tavern occupied by James Hartney, all on the east side of the Madawaska. Everything bore the aspect of ruin and desolation. The old-time glory of the place, if there ever was such a thing, had gone. In contrast the Madawaska River, its boiling white water, whirlpools and eddies, glistening in the sunlight, was beautiful in the implication it had conquered man's attempt at taming. This was the picture as McLachlin first saw it.

With the availability of timber it was possible to reconstruct the bridge and mills, but McLachlin had to consider the biggest problem of all, that of getting the timber to market. He had been considering the condition of the Buchanan constructed timber slide at the Chats along with other transportation problems. McLachlin had known of *The McNab* and the Buchanan brothers Andrew and George and their unsuccessful efforts to build a lumber industry in the village they had named. It is also thought possible that McLachlin, who at that time represented Bytown (now

Ottawa) in the Provincial Parliament, might have been made aware of the timber possibilities in McNab Township by Sir Francis Hincks one-time premier of the United Provinces of Upper and Lower Canada.

Although the journey from Bytown, where he operated a thriving lumber business and gristmill at Chaudiere Falls, was to check the potentiality of future timber and lumber possibilities on the Madawaska River and other tributaries of the Ottawa, McLachlin could not have visualized the impact this initial visit would ultimately have on the tiny village of Arnprior and the entire Upper Ottawa Valley encompassing both the Ontario and Quebec sides of the river. In 1846 the Union Forwarding & Railway Company was formed for the purpose of operating the steamers *"Emerald"* and *"Oregon"* and the building of a tram railway at the Chats to facilitate the transfer of passengers and freight from the lower sections of the Ottawa River to the upper. To make the trip from Bytown, research indicates McLachlin travelled by stagecoach to Aylmer, thence by the steamer *"Emerald"* to the village of Pontiac on the Quebec side of the Chats Rapids, then via the horse-operated tram railway from Pontiac to Union village at the head of the Chats, thence via the steamer *"Oregon"* to Arnprior.

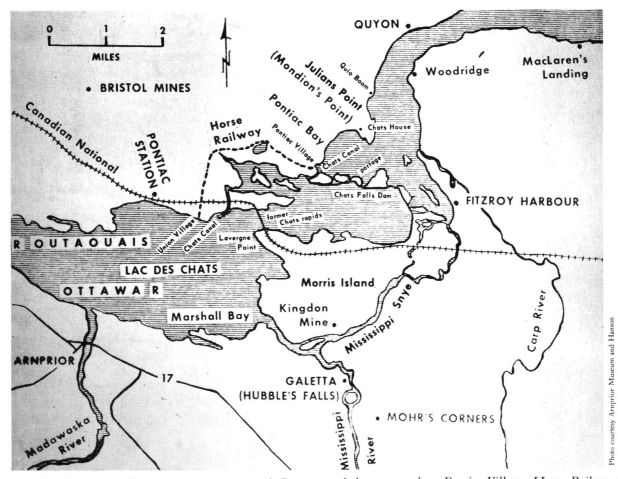

1851 route of Daniel McLachlin to Arnprior. Stagecoach Bytown to Aylmer, steamboat Pontiac Village, Horse Railway Union Village, Steamboat to Arnprior.

THE "GEORGE BUCHANAN"

A HISTORY OF Arnprior would not be complete without some reference to the early steamboat transportation on the Ottawa River and in particular that section known as Lac des Chats. Centuries ago in the year 1613, the great explorer Samuel de Champlain and his crew of *"coureurs de bois"* in their voyageur canoes, paddled up the Ottawa, portaged the many rapids including the wild and treacherous *"Chats"* and made their way to Arnprior. When McNab and the Buchanans arrived the canoe was still the primary means of travel in this region. Horseback, or on foot were the only alternatives.

And so in 1836 the steamer *"George Buchanan"* was built by Buchanan, William Mittleberger and James Simpson. The boat was constructed at Arnprior on the island midstream in the Madawaska River just below the present bridge. When the boat was ready for service Captain Daniel K. Cowley came to Arnprior from Lake Deschenes to take command of the new vessel. This was the pioneer steamer on Chats Lake, and she enjoyed a profitable career for many years.

The wood-burning boat was 95 feet in length, her beam 17 feet, and her hold seven feet in depth. She had guards six feet in width on each side for the paddle boxes and on these were the cookhouse, the mess, and other quarters. Her main deck was open from stem to stern. The engine room was on the starboard side near the guard. The boiler room, with its wood-fuelled boilers, was situated in the rear. Her average speed was seven miles per hour. Below were cabins, that for the ladies aft, and the main one twenty-four feet in length, with a table in the centre. Around the side were lockers topped with upholstered crimson colored cushions. The boat had a handsome bow with an ornamented figure-head, a bow sprit, cathead, capstan etc. In the stern were five windows. The boat operated for 18 years as a passenger and freight steamer.

COMPETITION

BY 1846 THE increased traffic on the Ottawa prompted John Egan and Joseph Aumond, lumbermen and merchants, to contract with the Molsons of Montreal for the construction of two iron steamers, one to ply upon Lake Deschenes, and the other on Chats Lake. Thus the steamers *"Emerald"* and *"Oregon"* came into being. The *"Emerald"* was assembled at Aylmer, while the *"Oregon"* was fitted up at Steen's Landing on the Mississippi River near Hubbell's Falls (now Galetta). Steamboats constructed later for operation on Lac des Chats will be dealt with as the McLachlin story unfolds.

McLACHLIN FAMILY

DANIEL McLACHLIN was one of thirteen children born to Scottish natives Hugh McLachlan (original spelling McLachlan changed to McLachlin by Daniel because of spelling variances in original) and his wife Janet McLean.

DANIEL McLACHLIN

The McLachlan patriarch, Hugh, was born in Corruaran, Kilmallie Parish, West Coast Scotland, in 1770. The family emigrated to Canada with four children in 1802 and settled at Riviere Rouge, Quebec, where they remained for twenty years prior to moving to St. Andrew's East, Rigaud Township. Hugh McLachlan, was the great, great grandfather of Norma Hall, and Eric Patterson (Pat) Hall, the last remaining descendants of this branch of the McLachlin family in the Arnprior area. Their mother was Norma McLachlin, daughter of Claude McLachlin.

The first Daniel was born in 1809 at St. Andrew's East. He worked for a while with his father who operated a barge forwarding business on the Ottawa River. It was at St. Andrew's that he met, fell in love with and married Maria Harrington also of St. Andrew's East. The young couple moved to Bytown where McLachlin, who seemed to possess the knack or adroitness to recognize possible profitable ventures, built a sawmill and gristmill at Chaudiere Falls in 1837. The couple had eight children, H. F. McLachlin, Claude, John, Daniel Jr. (not to be confused with the last Dan who was a son of H. F.) Eric, William, Jessie and Harriet. And so, Daniel McLachlin made his first visit to Arnprior. He didn't exactly like what he saw, but his keen foresight told him what he should do.

THE DECISION

NO SNAP DECISION was made, but neither was there a slow genesis. Daniel McLachlin was a smart businessman, marked by common sense and a clever discerning awareness and acumen. All problems, and possibilities of success, were well thought out before he made his final decision. McLachlin purchased the property, some 400 acres of land, and waterpower rights on the Madawaska watershed in what was known as Arnprior, Township of McNab, in 1851, from the Middleton firm in Liverpool.

Research would indicate that McLachlin made that trip of decision to Arnprior in 1851, but it is also thought there is the possibility that he had made a brief visit to this area prior to that year. Following acquisition of the holdings, McLachlin commenced the mammoth task of encouraging people to settle in the abandoned hamlet. To this end he had the property surveyed into town lots and in turn these were sold at a nominal figure, or given free of encumbrance, to those who could not afford to pay anything. In 1853 the bridge and dam were rebuilt with the assistance of the Hincks government. The old Buchanan sawmill, with one circular saw, located on the eastern extremity of the bridge, was renovated and put into operation. A stone gristmill was erected, something invaluable to the new settlers who at one time carried grain on their back to Bytown or Perth for milling. Laborers, mechanics and tradesmen were encouraged to settle in the newly resurrected village. The pine forests along the Madawaska adjacent to the village site resounded to the whack of the axe and the whining lament of the cross-cut saw, manned by husky, red-shirted shantymen. They felled giant white pines for square timber export and smaller ones to be used in building numerous log cabins as well as making repairs to the mills. The forest clear-cut on the site quickly gave place to stump dotted roadways criss-crossing the tiny settlement.

THE HILL

DANIEL McLACHLIN, in 1853, commenced construction of the baronial stone mansion to be known as *"The Hill"* at or very near the site of McNab's Kennell Lodge on the high bluff overlooking the Ottawa River. The McLachlin family moved from Bytown to Arnprior and their new home in 1857. Since that time the property has been held by four owners, the McLachlin family, R. M. Gemmel, Colonel W. H. Hadley, and the present owners, the Oblate Order of Mary Immaculate who purchased it in 1946.

Prior to the arrival of McLachlin, two Irishmen whose descendants became well known citizens of Arnprior, had settled near the land acquired by McLachlin. They were James Havey who, according to Belden's Historical Atlas, arrived on the scene in 1835 and whose descendants developed and still have extensive farm holdings here, and Hugh McGonigal who also continued residence and development of tracts of land in the area.

And going back even farther in history, Belden confirms timber operations actually in effect on the Madawaska in 1812 near what was to be the village of Arnprior. The Atlas describes the early lumbering operation this way: *"We have no record of the penetration of any white man into the forest gloom of this township prior to the year 1812, when the McConnell Brothers of Hull invaded its solitudes, and along the banks of the Madawaska, below the Flat Rapids, hewed the first square timber ever made on the Ottawa above the Chats Rapids. The spoilation of the forest proceeded for several years with greater or less activity, and the banks of the Madawaska were denuded of their choicest timber before the advent upon the scene of the pioneer settler. It is worthy of remark in this connection that the township under review is noted for having furnished some of the best timber ever secured on the Ottawa or its tributaries."*

McLachlin's entrepreneurial style of operation quickly won over the disillusioned Scottish immigrants who had been exploited by McNab. They were now ensured employment after their field crops had been sown. Work was available either in the sawmills or in the shanties that were relatively nearby at that early time.

In addition to encouraging people from the Bytown area to settle in Arnprior, the McLachlin enterprise attracted many immigrants from the old world. The potato famine in Ireland drove many people to Canada, in search of a new home; they came from France, Germany and Poland, and many of these immigrants settled in and around the village of Arnprior. Shantymen from Quebec also moved into the new lumber community.

Writing of McLachlin, Belden said, *"He immediately built extensive mills on the site of those destroyed by time and tempest, constructed the bridges which now span the river, and infused a vigorous vitality into the sleeping solitudes of the deserted village. The wand of a magician seemed called into play in the transformation that followed the arrival of McLachlin, but it was the magic of enterprise impelled by industry and liberality which wrought the change, and called a brisk village into being where only silence had reigned a few weeks previously."*

The first house, built in the business portion of the village during this second period of settlement, was erected near the corner of Elgin and Daniel Streets by Dennis McNamara. A general store followed, built by Andrew Russell and Son. Hotels were opened by Dennis McNamara, John Campbell and R. Lyon. Other business places quickly followed owned and operated by Eric Harrington, R. J. Whitelaw, one Farley, Brown and Wilson. The Post Office which had been managed by David Goodwin, a farmer, located a mile east of the village, was moved to the store of Andrew Russell who was appointed Postmaster. Russell had arrived in Arnprior in 1854. Schools and churches accompanied the village's advance. Amongst the various denominations at that time were Roman Catholic, Wesleyans, Presbyterian, Protestant Episcopal, Methodist Episcopal and Baptist.

THE HILL 1870

The village hummed and prospered, its growth almost phenomenal. The main streets, not much more than a stump-dotted sea of mud with board sidewalks pitted by the caulk marks of the log-drivers' boots, began to take some semblance of becoming a thoroughfare of the times. Two types of plank sidewalks were being constructed throughout the community. Those in the principal areas of heavy traffic were built of two-inch plank nailed crosswise on logs or timbers, while those for lesser traffic were planks laid lengthwise on the timbers, or *"sleepers"* as they were called. The boards were nailed with wrought iron square spikes which oftentimes loosened with the movement of the planks creating a hazardous situation often resulting in battered hands and knees.

Daniel McLachlin and his descendants were always known for their benevolence and goodwill towards their employees and the municipality. Numerous instances down through the years bear witness to this. Perhaps one of the more manifest is that following the death of Archibald McNab, it was learned that the Chief's widow held legal *"dower"* right. Mrs. McNab agreed to forego her claim by accepting 200 pounds sterling per year for life. McLachlin personally undertook to make this payment. Accordingly, from 1863 to 1868, the widow received pay-ments totalling over 1,100 pounds sterling until her death, when all claims expired.

Land for churches, institutions and various municipal projects was freely donated. And another story, one of many such, tells of the last Daniel McLachlin learning of the financial difficulties of an old retired employee, John Lajeunesse. To avoid embarrassment to Lajeunesse, McLachlin handled it thus — calling Lajeunesse into the office, McLachlin said, *"We were going over the books and found a mistake and we owe you $300."* McLachlin then handed over this amount to the elderly gentleman. A story also verified is that McLachlin loaned several hundred dollars to an employee to purchase a home. And there is no doubt that literally thousands of loads of firewood were given without charge to needy families throughout the community.

Two of the most historic events in the saga of Arnprior occurred in 1860, the occasion of the visit of the Prince of Wales (later King Edward VII) to Arnprior, and in 1864 when the first railway pushed its way to the tiny village thus solving the ever increasing transportation problems besetting the expanding McLachlin lumber operations. Two other very important events of more recent dates were the Old Boys' Reunion of 1909 and the Arnprior Centennial celebration of 1962.

CHARLES MACNAMARA

AS MENTIONED in acknowledgements at the outset of this narrative, much of the credit for historical matter in this book must go to the late Charles Macnamara and to his niece Jean Macnamara Cunningham who so graciously made available to the writer her uncle's files including historical writings and photographs of the McLachlin era. Charles Macnamara was born in Arnprior, the son of Richard Macnamara and his wife Richie Hannah Parnell. Richard emigrated to Canada and Quebec City with his parents in 1840 at the age of four years. The Macnamaras arrived on the Arnprior scene when H. F. McLachlin, one-time President of the McLachlin firm, went to Quebec and persuaded Richard Macnamara to come to Arnprior as the McLachlin office manager. Macnamara consented to the proposal; came to Arnprior taking up residence in the McLachlin built home on Daniel Street presently the heritage residence of his grand-daughter Jean Macnamara Cunningham. On July 2, 1881 he became Secretary-Treasurer of the company and worked at this position until July 1921 when he became ill and died on August 4 at the age of 86, after only two weeks illness.

Macnamara cabin, Marshall's Bay 1910. Left to right: Baptiste Charbonneau, Severe St. Jules, Eugene Grenier, Edward Diener, Henry Mallette and John Rowe.

Charles Macnamara went to work as accountant with McLachlin in 1886 immediately after graduating from High School at the age of 17. He later became Secretary-Treasurer remaining in that capacity until the company dissolved. He died in 1944. Charles Macnamara was a man of many interests. A keen naturalist and photographer, his comprehensive illustrated study of a beaver colony on the Ottawa River has been deposited in the Royal Ontario Museum. A number of excellent photographs are in the

Archives of Ontario. Macnamara was a familiar sight walking from his Madawaska Street home over the old *"Mill"* bridge and on through the Brown farm, the Goodwin's Bay area, to Marshall's Bay where he had a cottage and a tiny log cabin built in 1910 directly on the shores of Chats Lake by old-timers of the McLachlin firm. Over the front of the fireplace in the cabin is the Ojibway inscription, *"No-Pim-Ing Endad Ondji Ja-Wen-Imid"* translation *"The Dweller in the Woods is Always Happy"* presented to him by Lindsay Russell former Surveyor General for Canada. During the winter months Macnamara could be seen, snowshoes strapped to his back, walking out what is now highway 17 to the Brown farm where he would don the snowshoes and proceed on to his cabin. He appreciated beyond telling, the natural beauties of the forest and while in hospital during an illness he once said to his niece Jean, *"You don't have to go far away from home to find many interesting things."* Charles Macnamara was the driving force behind the institution of the Nopiming (Indian terminology for *"In the Woods"*) Game Preserve, which was declared a Game Sanctuary by Order in Council December 22, 1920 by the then Ontario Department of Game and Fisheries and the Provincial Government.

An historian of note, Macnamara had hoped to write a book about the McLachlin lumber industry but death intervened in 1944. Hopefully this historical document will, in some small way, pay well deserved credit to this man of Arnprior and the Valley.

Charles Macnamara's knowledge and dedication as a Naturalist and expert photographer has been rightfully recognized with the formation of a Naturalist organization bearing his name, the Macnamara Field Naturalists' Club.

VISIT OF THE PRINCE OF WALES

THE VISIT of the Prince of Wales to Arnprior on September 3, 1860 is perhaps the most historic visitation this community has ever experienced. Charles Macnamara, in 1939, wrote in detail of this as follows:

"An outstanding event in the history of Arnprior was the visit of the Prince of Wales (afterwards King Edward VII) to the village in 1860, where he was entertained by Daniel McLachlin at 'The Hill', Mr. McLachlin's fine residence overlooking the noble Ottawa River - 'la Grande Rivière' of the voyageurs. The visit took place early in September a day or two after the Prince had laid the cornerstone of the newly begun Parliament Buildings in Ottawa. Accompanied by the Duke of Newcastle, the Prince came by way of the steamboat 'Emerald' from Aylmer to the village of Pontiac at the foot of the Chats Rapids. Thence he journeyed by the horse-railway three and a half miles around the rapids to Lac des Chats. Here he was met by a fleet of bark canoes manned by rivermen in the employ of the several lumber firms on the Upper Ottawa. The men wore brightly colored shirts, vivid sashes around their waists, and white trousers.

Photo courtesy Jean Macnamara Cunningham

"The inevitable address was presented. It was written on birch bark and it was read from a specially prepared raft by Allan Mason, a foreman for Usborne & Company, lumbermen of Portage du Fort. Its text was mercifully short:

"'May it please Your Royal Highness, we, the raftsmen of the Upper Ottawa, who constitute a body of twenty thousand men, take advantage of meeting Your Highness on a 'deal' raft to express to you our loyalty and devotion to your Royal Mother, the Queen. Long may you remain the Prince of Wales.'"

The raftsmen were granted their wish. His Royal Highness the Prince did not become His Majesty the King until 41 years after this date. A steamboat was ready to convey the Royal party the three miles across the lake to the Arnprior wharf, but the 19 year old Prince naturally preferred to cross in a bark canoe, probably thereby adding another to the anxieties of the Duke of Newcastle. His Highness entered a canoe paddled by six McLachlin men, the names of two of whom have come down to us. One was Johnny Lajeunesse (great uncle of Arthur and Albert Grenier) a tall alert man, always happy and ready, known throughout the Valley as an expert riverman — in river parlance: 'a whitewater man and good on the loose'. Johnny had a fine voice, and going to Quebec on a raft, he usually got up a chorus among the men, which he led in singing the old French songs. The other canoeman remembered was John Vermette (grandfather of Leo, Kenneth and Alfred Vermette) who until his death in 1920 at the age of 87, was a respected citizen of Arnprior and a highly valued employee of McLachlin Brothers. John Vermette worked for the McLachlin family practically all his life, having begun as a chore boy for Daniel McLachlin and, in later years, was employed as a millwright and saw filer. He was always dignified and was endowed with the unaffected courtesy and good manners that seem to come naturally to many French Canadians: (there is also the probability that Joseph Desormia, as well as James McCormick, grandfather of Alex Staye, were part of the Royal canoe paddlers; also said to be a member of the flotilla was Thomas Havey, descendant of James Havey).

The paddlers belonging to the different firms wore different colored shirts and tradition has it that the McLachlin men were garbed in red.

A race soon began to see which canoe would reach the wharf first and the McLachlin *"red shirts"* were hard pressed by the blue shirted crew of another firm. The contest was keen and we can imagine how those powerful young rivermen plied their paddles. But at last the *"red shirts"* drew ahead of the *"blue shirts"* and the Prince's canoe came in first. It may well be that his crew won on their merits, for they were all picked men; but it is also possible that their success came from diplomacy on the part of the other crew. As the flotilla approached Arnprior a Royal salute was fired by R. W. Hardinge, a retired naval officer, from two small cannons that for many years after were familiar objects on the terrace in front of *"The Hill"*. Hardinge was the grandfather of Arnprior's Edgar Harrington Burwash. After

being entertained at lunch, the Prince graciously consented to plant an oak tree in *"The Hill"* grounds as a memorial of his visit. The tree, which had been prepared by George Fraser, McLachlin's head gardener, was planted with all ceremony. The sapling (of 124 years ago) known as the *"Prince's Oak"* now stands, a tall and sturdy tree overlooking Lac des Chats at what is now *"Galilee Community"* of the Oblate Order of Mary Immaculate.

The cloth on the lunch table and the chair the Prince sat in were long preserved at *"The Hill"* as historic relics. The chair is in the Arnprior Museum. And a large bark canoe, fastened with wooden pegs and lashed with *"watap"* (split roots of white spruce) and without a nail in its original construction, which was still in the possession of McLachlin Brothers in 1938, is thought to be the identical craft that bore the Prince across the Ottawa in 1860.

ROYAL OAK, THE HILL, 1902

Photo courtesy Ontario Archives and C. Macnamara Collection

After planting the tree the Prince drove to Almonte, the nearest railway station, in continuance of his tour of Canada. George Sutherland, then in McLachlin's employ and who in later years farmed on the 4th line of Fitzroy near Arnprior, was the Prince's coachman, and to the end of his life he was pointed out as *"the man who drove the Prince of Wales"*

It was estimated some 5000 people welcomed the Prince of Wales to Arnprior. They took up every conceivable vantage point to get a glimpse of the young Prince. One enterprising fellow, (like the Biblical story of Zacchaeus the rich tax collector, who being most anxious to see the kind of man Jesus was as He entered Jericho and, being a short man, he climbed a sycamore tree so as to get a good view) managed to get in close proximity to the Prince by climbing a tree directly over the Prince's head. Ordered down by a guard, he refused at first but a gun shoved to his head made him drop to the ground.

An old Irish lad, craning his neck to get a good look at the Prince, carelessly remarked, *"Shure he's only a sprig av a bye widout whuskers."* And along the road near Pakenham, an elderly lady stepped out into the road alongside the passing carriage and shouted, *"You're welcome to our country, Prince."* The Prince bowed to the lady, who, to her dying day, delighted to tell everybody that *"The Prince curtsied to me."*

The Royal canoe was 18 feet 6 inches long; 4 feet 3 inches wide amidships; and 1 foot 2 inches deep. Built of birch bark, no nails were used in its construction.

Royal Menu and Wine List, Prince of Wales visit to "The Hill" 1860.

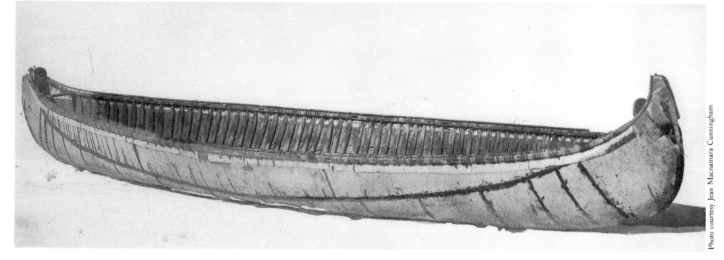

Photo courtesy Jean Macnamara Cunningham

Royal Canoe

VILLAGE INCORPORATED

SUCH WAS the boom in the tiny hamlet, that in July 1862 it was incorporated as a village with the following being elected members of the first village Council: Reeve, Eric Harrington; Daniel McLachlin, William Carss, James Havey, Thomas Toy. A. H. Dowswell was appointed Clerk and George Craig, Treasurer. Although it had ample population twenty years later to receive a town charter it was not until 1892 that Arnprior was incorporated as a town, at which time its population was about 3200. In a special section devoted to Arnprior, the Toronto Saturday Globe of October 1, 1892 said: *"Situated as it is at the confluence of the Madawaska and Ottawa Rivers, it not only has within its bounds all that* *should make it a manufacturing centre, but has also every inducement to offer as a health resort or a pleasant home."* Continuing the Globe said: *"Arnprior stands at the head of all the towns in the Dominion having less than 4,000 inhabitants for increase in its manufactured goods during the last decade; and second on the list as regards increase in population in the same length of time."* It was about this point in time that the McLachlin Brothers lumbering enterprise was said to be the largest manufacturer of sawn lumber on the North American continent. Back in 1863 there were 41 professional and business concerns in the community. A map of that era shows some of the principal streets as John, Elgin, Daniel, Victoria, Harriet, McGonigal, Hugh, Tierney, Peter and Patrick.

ARNPRIOR 1855

Photo courtesy Ontario Archives and E. P. Hall

THE GREAT RAILWAY CELEBRATION

ARNPRIOR AND THE lumber industry received a real *"shot in the arm"* on December 8, 1864, the date the Brockville & Ottawa Railway, subsequently the Canada Central, and later the Canadian Pacific Railway, rolled into Arnprior.

With the advent of the railway, McLachlin built his Number 1 sawmill at a point about centre of the bridge, and in the fall of that year commenced construction of mill Number 2 on the easterly end of the *"Mill"* bridge. Both these mills were water-powered. The coming of the railway, while not exactly the demise of the lake steamers, did curtail their activity to a great extent. But the new railway ensured even greater potential for the lumber industry and the development of Renfrew County and the Upper Ottawa. Typical of McLachlin, the event did not go unrecognized.

Thursday, December 8, 1864, heralded what was termed *"The Great Railway Celebration"* at Arnprior. While the name of the building in which the celebrations were held is not mentioned in old documents, records state it was in a *"large and commodious two-storey brick school"*. This no doubt was the Arnprior Public School situated on Ottawa Street where the present Walter Zadow School is located.

The dinner-dance was the most elaborate social event in the village since the visit of the Prince of Wales four years earlier. Hotels in town were crowded. Among the principal guests were J. G. Richardson, Managing Director of the B. & O. Railway; R. P. Cooke, the Railway's Chief Engineer; R. R. Smith, Warden United Counties Lanark and Renfrew, along with members of area Councils.

Chairman for the event was Daniel McLachlin who in his remarks said: *"Little did I once think we would ever have such a demonstration in Arnprior. When I first purchased Arnprior there was no talk of a railway; I found this place in a ruinous condition, with only one or two shattered and dilapidated houses and the ruins of Buchanan's mills; within the last few years I thought we never would see the railway here; but thanks to the energy and financial abilities of Mr. Richardson we are now celebrating its arrival and completion to Arnprior, and I hope it will not remain here, but that it will go forward and onward."*

Everyone likes to eat so they really dressed the menu which in those days was termed the *"Bill-of-Fare"*. Here it is: *"Turkeys, roasted and boiled; fowls variously dressed; Partridges; Wild Ducks; Geese; Prairie Hens; Roast Beef; Round of Beef; Hams; Tongues; Mutton Hams; Jellies;*

Public School, site of Great Railway Celebration 1864

Custards; Blanc Mange; Whips; Pineapples; Apples; Pears; Almonds; Raisins; Figs; along with the other various fruits." The wine and liquor list included: *"Champagne; Port; Sherry; Claret; Ale; Brandy; Rum; Scotch Whiskey, etc."*

And so McLachlin and Arnprior were on what would later be the main Trans-Canada line of the Canadian Pacific Railway. The lumber firm's transportation problems had come to an end. And in 1893, the Ottawa, Arnprior & Parry Sound came through to Arnprior. This was later known as the Canada Atlantic; Grand Trunk; and lastly the Canadian National Railway.

Some interesting information relative to the Brockville & Ottawa Railway appears in the George N. Tackabury 1876 Atlas. Tackabury states the original railway gauge was five feet six inches. This was changed in 1873 to the standard four feet eight inches and one half because of interchange problems with railway cars.

The B. & O. reached Arnprior, as mentioned, in 1864 and Sand Point about three years later. It was extended to Renfrew in 1872 and the company intended at that time to extend the railway to Pembroke in the years 1875 and 1876. By this time the timber located within a reasonable distance of Arnprior along the Madawaska River was well cut out and with it came the period of the *"shanties"*, first the *"Camboose"* and some years later the more modern lumber camp.

VILLAGE IN MOURNING

THE GREAT MAN was dead; the man who carved a destiny from the forests of the Upper Ottawa; the man who founded a dynasty that produced up to 60 million feet of lumber in a summer season to become the biggest manufacturer of sawn lumber on the North American Continent had died. February 6, 1872 was indeed a day of mourning in Arnprior, for on that day the pioneer builder of this village, the benevolent personage everyone trusted and loved, the first Daniel McLachlin died, just three years after his retirement. It was a solemn cortege that accompanied the body from *"The Hill"* where Rev. D. J. McLean conducted the service, to the graveside in the Arnprior cemetery, a location he had pointed out to his youngest son two years previous that he desired might be his last earthly abode. Perhaps the finest tribute to this man is inscribed on the Daniel McLachlin plaque erected by the Archaeological & Historic Sites Board of Ontario, near the spot where he first left the steamboat *"Oregon"* upon his arrival at Arnprior in 1851. It reads:

"One of the Ottawa Valley's most enterprising lumbermen, McLachlin was born in Rigaud Township, Lower Canada, and by 1837 had built a sawmill and gristmill at Bytown (Ottawa). In 1851, influenced by the timber potential of the Madawaska watershed, he purchased some 400 acres at the deserted hamlet of Arnprior and in 1854 laid out a town plot. The large sawmills which he built here greatly stimulated the community's growth. In the Legisla-

ture of the Province of Canada, McLachlin represented Bytown, 1851-54, and Renfrew County 1861-63. On Arnprior's incorporation in 1862 he was elected to the first village Council and he represented South Renfrew in the first Dominion parliament 1867-69."

His wife, Maria Harrington McLachlin, died July 20, 1897. The marble in the memorial to Daniel and Mrs. McLachlin was cut from the island just below the present bridge, shipped to Ottawa where it was fashioned and polished to become the tallest memorial in the Arnprior cemetery, a mememto to a man who stood very tall in the eyes of his peers throughout his lifetime.

DANIEL McLACHLIN PLAQUE

THE CAMBOOSE SHANTY

PERHAPS THE most authentic description ever compiled of the primitive *"camboose"* shanty and the later more modern lumber camp, is that by Charles Macnamara a few years before his death. It was an important phase in the history of Arnprior. Here it is as described by Macnamara.

"The modern lumber camp is a group of well constructed frame buildings, equipped and furnished much like a high class winter resort. In the dormitory there are separate spring beds with mattresses, sheets and blankets for each man; there is a separate wash room and often steam baths, a drying room for wet garments and a recreation room with reading matter and a radio. For a small weekly fee a laundress washes clothes. There are large airy dining rooms with well set tables, and the *"Bill-of-Fare"* in variety and excellence compares with that of a good hotel. The buildings are brightly lighted with gasoline lamps or electricity and are always comfortably heated by numerous stoves which special firemen attend day and night. Government regulations as to sanitation are strictly observed and even surpassed.

"In striking contrast to these luxurious establishments, here is an account of the old time 'camboose' shanty in universal use in early times and which survived in the Ottawa Valley up to about 1900.

"The typical '*camboose*' shanty that housed 50 to 60 was a low log building about 35 feet by 40 feet, with side walls six feet high and gables about 10 feet at the peak. Practically the only tools required to build it were axes and canthooks with some help from augers to bore sockets for posts and holes for dowel pins. No nails or spikes were used. The crevices between the logs were chinked with moss, the larger spaces being blocked with strips of wood. The building was roofed with '*scoops*', that is, logs hollowed out like troughs; and these scoops, supported by two long timbers ('*scoop bearers*') that stretched, 12 feet apart, from one gable to the other, were laid side by side, hollow side up, sloping from the low peak to the eaves. The joints between them were covered with other scoops turned hollow side down, and the ridge of the roof, where the scoops butted together, was also covered with inverted scoops. The close-by horse stable and the combined granary and meat house were built in the same way.

"The sole entrance to the shanty was a rather small door in one end of the building, about six feet high and three feet wide. Rarely there was a window some two feet square at the cook's table; and very occasionally the clerk had a small opening in the logs to illumine his rude desk. But as a rule there were no windows at all, and all the light and ventillation (not so much light but lots of ventilation) came through a large hole in the roof, 12 feet square, surrounded by a square chimney of flatted timber five or six feet high and tapered to about eight feet square at the top. Besides letting in light and air, this opening carried off the smoke of the '*camboose*' which all important institution will be described more particularly later.

"The inside plan of a shanty was not always exactly the same, but the following was a common arrangement. The floor was of flatter timber not very closely fitted, and the spaces between the pieces soon filled up with rubbish. To the right of the door as you came in was a pile of four foot firewood. The hardworking chore boy had to provide about a cord and half every 24 hours, as well as six large

Camboose Shanty, Lake Travers, 1901. Paul Kittner camp cook.

'back logs'. In front of the door, between it and the 'camboose' was the place of the grindstones, usually two, which in the evening were in constant use sharpening axes. If square timber was being made as well as sawlogs, there was a third stone for the broad axes, which need a flat-faced stone to grind them, and narrow axes hollowed out the stone. To the left of the door were two barrels of wash water for the men and a stand for a couple of wash basins. There was a spout through the logs here to empty out the dirty water. It often froze up in winter and the ice had to be forcibly punched out.

"Next in the corner stood the cook's water barrel, and along the left wall came the cook's shelf for meat and other stores, the cook's work table and the bread shelf. Farther along this side the clerk had his desk and beside it the van chest which held the tobacco, moccasins, clothing and sundries for sale to the men. The right side of the building was all taken up by two tiers of bunks, six or seven in each tier and across the end farthest from the door were two more tiers of seven bunks each, in which the men slept with their feet to the fire. Continuing down the left wall, before you came to the clerk's outfit, there might be four more bunks and this was where the foreman slept. Often his was the only bunk in this corner. A bench of flatted timber resting on blocks extended all along in front of the bunks.

"The bunks were floored with flatted poles and the bedding was usually balsam boughs, sometimes hay. Each man was supplied with a pair of heavy grey wool blankets and two men slept together. A properly made balsam bed is quite comfortable; and as the men took off no more than their moccasins on retiring, when covered with their two pairs of blankets they were warm enough, despite the large opening in the roof, even in the coldest weather. It was not unusual for visitors to ask if the hole was not closed at night, much to the amusement of the shantymen.

"And now for the 'camboose', the heart of the shanty (French: cambuse, provision room or shipboard). It was a square of logs in the middle of the shanty, 12 feet each way, retaining a foot or so of earth and sand, on which a

The Camboose

fire for heating and cooking burned day and night. Four posts at the four corners rose to the low roof and to one of them was attached the cramier (French: crémaillère), the ingenious adjustable crane that swung the pots over the fire. One end of the 'camboose' was divided off by a log into a separate trough filled with sand. In this place, known as the 'bean poles' beans and bread were baked in cast iron kettles buried in the hot sand. The 'cook's shovel' used to bury the kettles was round-pointed with a short socket into which the cook fitted a long straight handle. In the hardware trade the implement was known as an 'Irish miner's shovel' The 'cookery' consisted of about four camp kettles, large iron pots of 10 or 12 gallons with bails and tin covers, seven or eight bake kettles, cast iron 'ovens' 14 inches to 16 inches in diameter and four to five inches deep with cast iron covers and lugs, a five gallon tin tea pail and a large dish pan. Other appliances were several pairs of pot hooks of various sizes to handle the kettles and pots. What might be called the tableware if there had been any table — but there wasn't — were tea dishes (pannikins), tin plates and soup spoons. No knives or forks were provided. Each man bought a small butcher knife, and the experienced shantyman used it with neatness and dexterity. Between meals it was stuck in the wall of the owner's bunk.

"At night the 'camboose' fire supplied the only light. There were no lamps, except that the clerk might bring a small lamp from home for his desk and get an odd bottle of oil from the depot. Even the teamsters had no lanterns. About every Saturday the cook and chore boy rendered beef tallow and cast thick short yellow candles in a tin mould. The teamsters made holders by winding hay wire (the shantyman's ever ready help in time of trouble) around a broom handle to a depth of four or five inches and slipping the coil off. This was fastened to the scoop bearer between the horses and the candle dropped into it. Actually, the 'camboose' fire lit up the shanty better than lamps could have. It was as large and cheerful as a good sized bonfire and it never went out. A French Canadian shantyman said to me once: 'At night we sit on the bench around the fire and everyone is gay.' If it got low in the night there was always someone to throw on a stick of cordwood; and the cook began his day at anything between three and four in the morning. Early to bed was the rule. Eight o'clock was a late hour in the shanty. Everyone had to be at his place of work by break of day, and the farther he had to go the earlier he started. He stayed on the job until sundown and then walked back, often several miles to the shanty. I have heard a shanty philosopher expressing doubts as to the whole truth of the proverb about early to bed and early to rise. 'I have been doing that all my life,' he said, 'and I'm healthy enough, but I don't know about being wise, and I'm sure not wealthy.'

"The 'camboose' shanty was the old original cafeteria. There was no table and everyone served himself. Getting a tea dish, a tin plate and a hunk of bread from the cook's shelves, the hungry man took whatever food he wanted from the pots and kettles around the fire; then, sitting on the bench with his brimming tea dish beside him and his heaped plate on his knee, he proceeded to eat with the ready help of his butcher knife. For the perfection of hospitality you had to come to the 'camboose'. Food was always ready; no one pressed you to eat and no one stopped you. You ate as much as you pleased and at any time. Some even got up in the middle of the night for a snack. No wayfarer was ever refused food and to charge for a meal was something unheard of.

"With his simple open fire and his few pots and kettles, it was surprising what well prepared food the 'camboose' cook could set out. All his dishes were fine examples of good plain cooking and the bread baked in the sand was particularly fine. It was close-grained yet light and of a delectable nutty flavor. The latest electric ovens of these days produce nothing better — if as good. The bread was raised with dried yeast cakes, which are yeast cells mixed with flour. Growth was started on mashed potatoes and — though the cook did not know exactly why — an infusion of hops was added to prevent the growth of bacteria and moulds. Some of the older cooks often used leaven to raise their bread, that is, dough that has fermented or 'gone sour'. The leavened bread usually had a sour taste and oldtimers have told me that they became so used to the flavor that they did not relish the yeast bread they got at home.

"While the food was unlimited in quantity and excellent in quality, it was lacking in variety. Now-a-days the Bill-of-Fare would be condemned as wanting in essential vitamins. Nevertheless shantymen were an exceptionally healthy and vigorous race. They rarely suffered from anything that could not be cured by a few pills or a bottle of Pain Killer. And they worked harder and for much longer hours than anyone does in these eight hour days. There cannot have been much wrong with their nourishment.

"Breakfast was always about the same; baked beans, bread and tea, green tea; black tea and coffee were never used. Some liked to add a little black strap molasses to their beans.

"At noon most of the men were working far out in the bush and only the few who might be close to the shanty came in for dinner. They had a choice of breakfast beans warmed over, cold salt pork or boiled fresh beef (salt beef and mutton were never seen in the shanties), bread, dried applies, and perhaps molasses or corn syrup; and of course boiling hot tea, which was said to be just right when it was strong enough to float an axe. At one time sugar was a rare luxury but later 'No. 1 Yellow' was always on hand.

"Each gang working together in the woods; logmakers, road cutters, teamster, skidder, took a lunch with them in a cotton bag. It consisted simply of boiled salt pork — very fat Chicago heavy mess — and bread and tea. A wise precaution was to bury the lunch bag in the snow to hide it from the ravens who liked nothing better than to tear it open with their powerful beaks and devour the lunch. The French Canadians interpreted the bird's hoarse croak as 'poche, poche' (bag, bag) and said he was calling for the lunch bag. At noon the men sat around a camp fire and boiled their tea and sometimes had to thaw out the bread by holding it on a stick close to the flame. The teamster gave his horses their oats and the men ate the fat pork and smoked their pipes a while before going back to work. This sounds like frugal fare but I have seldom enjoyed a meal as much as the bread and pork at a logmaker's fire in the winter woods.

"Supper was the principal meal of the day. The main course was a camp kettle full of boiled beef and another of boiled potatoes. Salt pork also was available; and dessert would be represented by boiled rice with raisins and stewed dried apples flavored with cinnamon. These were the real old brown apples that had been dried in quarters on cotton strings and tasted much beter than the bleached evaporated apples introduced later. There was always unlimited bread and sometimes rather high flavored butter. Sea pie was the special treat on Sunday morning. A couple of bake kettles were filled with pork, beef, bread and dough with plenty of fat and buried in the hot sand to bake. Old shantymen lick their lips when they think of sea pie. Another Sunday special was 'des grillades', mess pork cut into slices and fried. This was very good eating but it was considered a wasteful way of cooking pork, higher authorities did not approve of it. The hiring agreement that the men were supposed to sign — and never did — stipulated for 'usual shanty board with the exception of fried pork'. However, the exception was often ignored. Once in a while pea soup was served; and if there was any baking powder, the cook would make a batch of enormous cookies the size of a tea plate. They were tasty enough but not what you might call rich. Also there was generally a barrel of shanty biscuit (hardtack) on hand for use before the cook got his bread baked, or in emergencies and on journeys.

"Compared with modern ways of living, life in the 'camboose' shanty may seem to have been rough and hard. Contrasted with the general conditions of the time, the difference was not so great. In those days, waterworks and toilet conveniences were unknown outside of the large cities, the wonders of electricity in our homes were still in the future, houses were mostly heated with wood stoves, and when you woke up on a cold winter morning you were apt to find the water in your room frozen solid. The never dying fire on the 'camboose' was kindlier than that.

"In general the men were satisfied with their lot and their work and did not think that they were suffering any particular hardships. They felt at home in the shanty and enjoyed the freedom of the life. Yet there was a code of conduct and even rules of etiquette to which the newcomer had to conform or he was soon 'given his time' and sent down. The men who did not fit in were eliminated and the gang settled down for the winter as a more or less harmonious community, only a little disturbed when hired teams came in at New Year's. They were content to be largely cut off from the outside world until the creeks began to break up in the Spring and it was time to get the rigging for the drive ready.

"In preparing this article," said Macnamara, "I have been greatly helped by my old friends, George L. Graham and Charles Kerr of Arnprior. I was only an occasional visitor to the shanties, while my friends spent many long years in them and are familiar with every detail of life and work in the woods. Their testimony is, that with all its drawbacks, the 'camboose' shanty was a pretty good place to live in after all."

GEORGE L. GRAHAM

GEORGE GRAHAM was a long time clerk, bookkeeper and agent for McLachlin Brothers from January 1892 until the final cleanup on the Kipawa and Black Rivers in 1938. He kept a detailed record of the amount of timber taken out of each camp and of the quantity of supplies supplied for each particular camp. An example is the season of 1898-99 in the Simon Kelly camp. They produced 30,331 pieces white pine logs totalling 3,515,140 board measure; 1088 pieces red pine logs 108,056 board measure; 225 pieces spruce logs 28,738 board measure. 48 pieces shingle block 5,326 board measure; and 192 pieces boom timber 48,685 board measure for a total of 31,884 pieces equalling 3,705,945 feet board measure. His supplies for this camp were, from August 20, 1898 to April 29, 1899 as follows: 69 tons of hay; 3366 bushel oats; 83 barrels flour; 30 barrels pork; 42 bushels beans; 22 head of cattle; 3652 lbs. dressed beef; 7183 lbs. bacon; 192 bags potatoes; 1204 lbs. butter; 504 lbs. cheese; 616 lbs. green tea (one can boil and leave green tea on stove all day long — one brand was called gun-powder); 2565 lbs. sugar; 496 lbs. syrup; 1084 lbs. apples; 308 lbs. rice; 224 lbs. raisins; 690 lbs. salt; 29 lbs. pepper; 3 lbs. ginger; 7 lbs. hops; 65 lbs. biscuit; 182 head cabbages; 16 bags cabbages; 23 bags turnips; 408 lbs. whitefish; 220 lbs. mince meat; 21 lbs. soda; 10 gallons coal oil; 4 boxes soap; 7 lbs. baking powder; 2 barrels sauerkraut; 10 bags carrots; 120 lbs. cod fish.

Pointer Boat, mouth of Madawaska, G. Graham in bow

Photo courtesy Stewart Graham, C. Macnamara collection

Charles Macnamara has seen every phase of a lumbering operation from the old *"camboose"* days to the modern lumber camp, the square timber drives to Quebec City and the log drives down the Madawaska, Bonnechere, Kipawa, Black, Coulonge and Petawawa Rivers to the Upper Ottawa where they were taken over by the Upper Ottawa Improvement Company, an association of all the principal Ottawa Valley operators. Familiarly known as the *"I.C.O."* this company was authorized to charge the log owners sufficient to cover expenses and to pay an annual dividend not exceeding ten percent on the capital stock.

THE SQUARE TIMBER

IT IS FROM this scenario as envisaged by Macnamara that many incidents in the once great McLachlin Brothers lumber camps unfold. In 1885-86 when Macnamara began working with McLachlins the square timber trade was drawing to its end with the company taking out only two or three rafts after that time. The early square timber era of the Upper Ottawa came at a time when England required much wood not only for housing but for its immense ship building program. During the Napoleonic wars the Baltic Sea was sealed off for a time preventing access to the rich forest resources in that area and there is the theory that Britain, because of this, resorted to the new world for large quantities of timber for ship building and the making of ship's masts. The square timber was floated down the tributaries of the Ottawa, then rafted together and carried on down the Ottawa to the St. Lawrence and on to Quebec City where it was loaded into ocean going vessels. At each rapid the main raft was dismantled and divided into cribs for shooting the rapids by way of the timber slides.

Square Timber

Photo courtesy E. P. Hall

A timber raft contained 80,000 to 120,000 cubic feet of white pine. A raft was composed of up to 100 cribs, and the individual timbers were 40 feet or more in length. Each crib was of standard size so as to facilitate movement through the various timber slides. The raft foreman was called the *"Pilot"* and the crew lived on the raft. Propulsion was by sails and when the raft was stalled in a calm the crew used a unique method of proceeding. The raft was equipped with a winch and cable; a boat would carry the cable, to which was attached a heavy anchor, some distance forward and drop anchor. Then the raftsmen winched the raft forward. One of the last rafts on the Ottawa river was in 1903. David A. Gillies was on board this raft to Quebec City. Gillies also travelled on a raft down the Trent River to Lake Ontario, the St. Lawrence River and on the Quebec.

THE WOODS

ACCORDING TO Charles Macnamara the first stir in the old time shanty year was the forwarding of horses from Arnprior in September. These were horses that had come down in the Spring with their ribs showing after a winter's work but had been pasturing all summer on the green fields of the Brown farm and the Hartney farm. Macnamara said it was curious to see how the pairs of horses that had worked together all winter still kept up their companionship in the summer and grazed side by side in the pastures. A few of the teams were harnessed to heavy wagons and the rest of the horses were led on halters. The wagons carried oats and harness, and a few supplies but the bulk of the supplies were drawn on sleighs in the winter. The standard for each man was a seamless cotton flour sack stuffed with clothes, known to the English speaking fellows as a *"turkey"* while the French called it *"poche de butin"* or *"bag of booty"*. The wagons had to be strongly built as roads were unbelievably bad. The driver's seat was fitted with spring poles to ease the shocks but a small man was in danger of being bounced off, and Charlie Pell, who answered that description, used to strap himself on.

Teamsters were not trusted with money to pay expenses as many would spend it for booze at the first stopping place. They were given written *"way orders"* to present at stopping places. In winter a frame sleigh, with eight strong stakes about five feet long set along the sides in holes in the frame, was the transportation. The stakes were hammered in hard so that they could not easily be pulled out, all but one stake which was left loose in its socket. This loose stake was known only to the teamster and if a fight started he grabbed it from the socket and waded in.

Provisions and equipment for a shanty were drawn in on snow roads in the winter for use the following year. Before the shanty gang arrived these stores were in charge of a *"keepover"* man. The *"keepover"* man was often kept busy shovelling over oats to prevent them from moulding and upending sacks of flour so the contents would not cake. Barrels of pork sometimes needed re-brining; these were often buried in the earth to protect them from the summer heat.

Before the Ottawa, Arnprior & Parry Sound Railway was built through the lumber country, large quantities of shanty supplies were assembled at Arnprior and forwarded from there by horse and wagon or sleigh to the various shanties on the Madawaska and Bonnechere Rivers. The Opeongo Road was perhaps the best known highway of that day. In the heyday of lumbering, McLachlin Brothers pork order every year was 1,000 barrels of Chicago heavy mess, which arrived in November or December in one shipment of ten carloads. There were also carloads of beans, flour, sugar, syrup and numerous other groceries. The yearly purchases of hay ran into hundreds of tons and of oats into thousands of bushels, mostly bought from settlers near the shanties.

THE SHANTYMAN

THE FIRST shanty gangs were sent up in early September. They came from all points; Arnprior, White Lake, Burnstown, Springtown, Calabogie, Renfrew and Eganville. Mount St. Patrick was noted for its tall Irishmen. But the bulk of the hiring was done in Bytown (Ottawa). The principal shantymen's hotels were on Murray Street with others on Clarence, Water and Sussex Streets. Here gathered men from all over Eastern Ontario and a large part of the Province of Quebec to look for work in the vast forests of the Ottawa Valley.

The hotel keepers did a lot of the hiring. When the gang was ready to leave, they were loaded into express wagons and driven down to the C.P.R. station at the Flats. Many were more or less drunk, with bottles sticking out of hip pockets. A shanty gang on the way to the bush was not a welcome sight to a train conductor, but to keep order there was always an able bodied crew member or two on board, well used to rough and tumble fighting. Macnamara on one such trip mentions that the shantymen recognized him as "le comis" second in rank only to "le bourgeois". He was treated with a certain amount of respect; but nothing like that shown a priest passing through the crowded boisterous car. Way was instantly made for him and hats were touched obsequiously when they were not taken right off.

There was a certain amount of competition amongst the lumber people when hiring shantymen. Macnamara describes how one McLachlin foreman, Evariste Nadeau, "a good-looking man of medium height, broad shouldered and strong, quiet spoken but a wicked fighter when roused", handled such a situation. Nadeau was smoking quietly in Renaud's Hotel on Murray Street when three fine looking young French Canadians whom he had been trying to hire came in and said they had decided to go up for Gillies on the Coulonge. This was a disappointment for Nadeau but he continued smoking and said nothing for a minute or two. Then he remarked: "Yes, I have been up to Gillies limit on the Coulonge. It takes you a week to get there and for three days you wade to your waist in water pulling boats

up the rapids." When the McLachlin limits were all on the Madawaska and Bonnechere, the men went by train to Cobden, stayed overnight at John McCoy's hotel and took the stagecoach next day to their destination. Another noted stopping place was Payette's at Brudenell.

By 1900 the "camboose" shanties had gone. Macnamara made his first trip to Black River where he spent two weeks with Dan and Hugh McLachlin. He lugged around his Premo camera taking many photographs of the works. One of the "camboose" shanty cooks was Paul Kittner who died at Arnprior in 1940.

If one ever wondered how a lumber company arrived at the amount of food to store for a lumber camp, this is one method used by McLachlins. The following is the consumption of one man for one day on the Black River limit in 1900-01. The figures include waste and do not give the actual amount a man ate every day. The quantities, multiplied by the number of men in the shanty and by the number of days it was expected the shanty would operate, gave the quantity of provisions to be laid in.

Flour	1.24 lbs.
Potatoes	1.14 lbs.
Pork and Bacon	1.04 lbs.
Beef	.89 lbs.
Beans	.24 lbs.
Sugar	.23 lbs.
Raisins	.03 lbs.
Syrup	.06 lbs.
Butter	.08 lbs.
Tea	.05 lbs.
Apples	.06 lbs.
Peas	.01 lbs.
Rice	.03 lbs.
Cheese	.04 lbs.
Jam	.09 lbs.

Shantymen were sometimes belittled by so-called snobs. Macnamara describes Tom Yuill telling him, "that the simpering Miss Galligan of Renfrew said at a social gathering: 'You know, I am always ashamed to tell anyone that my father was a shanty cook'. Bob Powell, noted native wit replied: 'Ah yes, Ma'am, he **was** a damned bad cook."

The Black River depot buildings were on a hillside overlooking Lake Travers. The log houses were comfortable, clean and tidy, although there was not a woman around the place. A woman at a lumber depot was unheard of in those days. Years later a depot clerk was allowed to bring his wife to Lake Travers. Macnamara mentioned that when Kenneth McLachlin was at Black River the depot cook was Pierre Pelletier, an excellent cook but rather eccentric. He once punched the eyes out of the picture of a man someone had put on the wall because, he said, it watched him wherever he went. When Kenneth announced his intention of going home in a few days, Pelletier the next morning came into his room before he was up and began collecting his soiled clothes which it was his usual job to wash. Kenneth said: "Oh never mind those, Pierre, I'll get them washed at home." Pierre was indignant, *"I will not let you take all those things home that way and have your mother call me a dirty son of a bitch."* Closing his remarks on the Black River, Macnamara says, *"how vividly a smell will sometimes awaken long forgotten memories — whenever I smell wood smoke on a cold winter night, suddenly I am back at Black River depot crossing the wooden walk between the office and the cook house, with the northern stars hanging in the sky over Lake Travers, the Big Bear swinging lowest of all."*

THE LOGMAKERS

LOGMAKERS WERE the highest paid men in the shanty. In Ontario, logmakers were required to keep count of how many logs they made each day and report the number at night to the clerk for entry in a book furnished by the Government. At the end of the season the clerk was supposed to take an affidavit to the correctness of this record. It was seldom correct and nearly always differed from the count of logs measured by the culler. The logmakers were illiterate and depended on their memory and were apt to exaggerate their work. There was also the strong suspicion that the clerk did not always go to the trouble of entering up the book every night but just *"cooked"* it up in the Spring. The difficulty was that if the total of the Government book was larger than the culler's count, the Government would charge stumpage on the greater amount, taking the word of the careless, irresponsible logmaker, in preference to the sworn record of the professional culler.

Photo courtesy Ontario Archives, C. Macnamara collection

Log Skidders 1900

Log Makers 1900

Photo courtesy Ontario Archives, C. Macnamara collection

THE ROADCUTTERS

ROADCUTTERS MIGHT be called apprentice shantymen. At this he learned to use an axe. There were two kinds of these workers — road cutters and main road cutters. The first cleared narrow trails for the teamster to drag out the logs from where they were cut to the rollway; the second cut roads wide enough for the sleighs that drew the logs from the rollway to the lake or stream where they were laid on the ice. Red pines are *"intolerant"* trees and permit very little growth beneath their shade. When lumbering in a stand of red pine the road cutters may have little to do. So little in fact, that Macnamara states McLachlin Superintendent Armon Burwash once told him, *"the only way the teamsters could tell where the roadcutters had gone was by tobacco spits on the snow."*

LOG MARKS

ON ALL McLACHLIN logs the hammer mark, $\mathcal{N}$ was made on the end of a log with a large cast iron hammer bearing the raised characters. The numeral indicated the limit and shanty, so it was always possible to tell where any log had come from.

Bark marks were also placed on logs. The McLachlin bark mark was three blazes around the log with the monogram $\mathcal{N}$ inscribed on each blaze. Their logs were easily identified at sorting gaps. Gillies Brothers "V" hammer mark and IXXI on 2 sides of a log with inverted T, P or C, signifying Temagami, Petawawa or Coulonge limit cut into the "V". E. B. Eddy mark was the letter "N". The J. R. Booth bark mark was the mud turtle, represented by a large blaze with two chips removed at either end for the legs.

LAKE TRAVERS ON THE BLACK RIVER

LIQUOR WAS strictly forbidden in the shanties and the rule was well enforced. Pain Killer was one of the standard medicines on the shelf in the Depot Clerk's office. The stuff was said to be compounded of high wines and cayenne pepper, and was much used by men getting over a drunken spree on the way up. Occasionally it might be noticed that a cook was using an unusually large quantity of raisins and when his activities were investigated, he would be found to be making *"poteen"*. Macnamara remembers H. F. McLachlin telling him that one John Dennison, a handyman on the Madawaska, was in the habit of making whiskey in his shop, but H. F. said *"as Dennison drank the liquor all himself, it did not do much harm"*. McLachlin described one incident when a foreman discovered that a gang of his men were drinking in a wayside cabin instead of working, and had become quarrelsome. The liquor was in a tin pail on a trestle table and the men were sitting around drinking from tea dishes. The foreman put on a pair of deerskin moccasins so that he would be able to run well and went to the cabin. He opened wide the door and leaving it open behind him, jumped in and kicked over the table, spilling the liquor on the ground. Then he dashed out and ran down the road at full speed for eight miles without stopping.

THE STOVE COOK

THE STOVE COOK soon displaced the *"camboose"* cook and in a short time it was difficult to find a man who knew how to cook in the sand. The Bill-of-Fare was enlarged with the better cooking facilities. Pies and cakes appeared on the table. The men helped themselves, à la cafeteria.

Shantymen were always well fed, many of them better than they were at home. Macnamara tells how he once heard Tom Carpenter swearing at Gaspé men who raised some objection to the food. *"Damn them, and all they get to eat at home is cod's heads."* The cod fish itself was too valuable for home consumption.

No one in the bush, except a teamster, ever wore an overcoat. Bill Lampole, patriarch of prominent Arnprior families, was one of McLachlin Brothers teamsters and, of course, wore an overcoat. Work with axe and peavey could not be carried on in an overcoat and besides these workers were in the sheltered bush. But the teamster, sitting on his load, had to cross wide lakes and come out into wind-swept places, so he wore a coat.

THE BEEF-SKIN MOCCASIN

TYPICAL DRESS of a shantyman in Fall or early Winter was, felt hat, heavy flannel shirt, vest, no coat, heavy trousers and beef-skin moccasins. Beef moccasins were the universal footwear in the woods though often replaced in cold weather by deer-skin moccasins. The *"souliers de boeuf"* originated with the French Canadians. The traditional winter dress of the Quebec habitant was a *"bonnet rouge"* or touque, long skirted coat tied around the waist with a sash and *"souliers de boeuf"*. The old beef moccasins came in short and long types and the long moccasins came up to the knee. They were as hard as a board and to soften them they were hung up and filled with warm water and soaked overnight. When the water made them flexible they were coated with neatsfoot oil or fish oil making them reasonably waterproof and soft. Later the *"oil-tanned"* moccasins were brought on the market. These did not need preliminary softening and oiling. Beef moccasins were messy, smelly things and soon disappeared, supplanted by rubber footwear.

PETER TAIT AND THE OLD STOREHOUSE

DEMOLISHED IN 1938 the old storehouse on the east side of the Madawaska River, built in the 1840's, was one of the oldest buildings in Arnprior. It was originally an hotel and when McLachlin came to Arnprior in 1851 the hotel was operated by James Hartney. Mrs. Nathaniel Burwash stayed in the hotel when

Photo courtesy Ontario Archives, C. Macnamara collection

Black River 1903, Bill Lampole in overcoat

Photo courtesy Ontario Archives, C. Macnamara collection

Log maker's lunch, Black River 1903

as a young woman, she came to Arnprior with her husband in 1854. Her arrival was at night and she said when she looked out of the hotel window in the morning all she could see was a corduroy road and cedar swamp. In its day the old hotel was the scene of many fights between factions of shantymen, raftsmen and local farmers.

Now to Peter Tait, a storeman for McLachlins from 1883 until the mills closed in 1929. In his younger days Tait had been a teamster to the Black Hills in the gold rush. He told many stories of happenings there in the days of Wild Bill Hickok and Calamity Jane and the Deadwood Coach. He was one of those old-time story tellers the like of which is rarely seen in these 1980's.

Old storehouse 1900, one time Hartney Hotel and Tavern 1851

Photo courtesy Ontario Archives, C. Macnamara collection

THE RIVERMEN'S POINTER

THESE BOATS were called *"bonnes"*, perhaps with the idea that they were *"bonnes-à-tout-faire"*. They were painted red and ranged in size from about 20 feet to 60 feet. Boat builder's price for them was one dollar per foot. In later years McLachlins built their boats in their own shop and the men were so well organized that a boat begun in early morning was ready to be painted at four o'clock in the afternoon. The McLachlin *"pointers"*, built in their wagon shop, were of three lengths, 22 foot, 35 foot and 40 footers. All were equipped with oar locks for two pairs, three pairs or four pairs of oars. The 22 footers were used primarily for light jobs requiring quick maneuverability, the larger for moving camps from one site to another. They built as many as 47 *"pointers"* in one year. A vital part of the boat were the so-called *"knees"* or ribs, two inches thick, used to hold the sides and bottom together. Always of eastern cedar, the McLachlin men would scour area farms in search of cedar stumps, from which the curved *"knees"* were made. Camps were set up in a stump dotted field, men with axes, assisted by horses, would haul out the stumps. The *"pointer"* was built with the best white pine lumber from the air-dried piles. The

seams were caulked with oakum, a jute fibre impregnated with tar, then finished with white, or red lead of putty-like consistency. The boats were always painted a bright signal red. Old-time McLachlin employees Eugene Grenier and son Arthur were part of a crew of McLachlin boat builders. Arthur Grenier built the last *"pointer"* boat from a McLachlin Brothers pattern which he had in his possession.

THE OPEONGO ROAD

ALMOST EVERYONE has heard of the *"Opeongo Road"*. The *"Opeongo Road"* was surveyed as a colonization road and farm lots were laid off on each side of it. On the map it appears as a broad ribbon from Lake Clear to Bark Lake, a rough, rocky, hilly country. According to old maps it was originally projected from the mouth of the Bonnechere River. The *"Opeongo Road"* was everything that a road should not be and the name meant everything primitive and backward in farming.

THE MILLS

FOR IDENTIFICATION purposes and in chronological order McLachlins named their sawmills Numbers 1, 2, 3 and 4. Following reconstruction of the *"Mill"* bridge in 1853, Daniel McLachlin renovated the old Buchanan mill on the east bank of the Madawaska and operated this for some years. About 1862 he built the water-powered No. 1 sawmill near centre of the bridge. Equipment in this mill consisted of one stock gate, one slabber and two Yankee gates. McLachlin then proceeded with the construction of a second and larger mill near the eastern extremity of the bridge, completing this in the Autumn of 1862. Known as No. 2 mill, it was equipped with one stock gate, one slabber, one large circular saw, with all necessary edgers, trimmers and appliances for the manufacture of lath. The massive stone foundations of mill No. 2 were demolished in 1973 when Ontario Hydro commenced construction of the present four lane bridge and weir.

Although the first Daniel McLachlin retired in 1869 there is no doubt that his enterprising spirit still prevailed as his sons, Hugh F. (always known as H. F.), John, Daniel Jr., and later the youngest son, Claude, assumed management of the company. A third mill operated by steam, and known as No. 3 was built in 1871 on the shore of Chats Lake. After running successfully for four years it was destroyed by fire. It was immediately replaced by a new steam mill, also known as No. 3, described by the Toronto Saturday Globe of October 1, 1892, as *"for size and cutting capacity stands at the head of its kind on the continent"*. A fourth sawmill, also steam operated, and known as No. 4, was built in 1892 a few hundred yards east of No. 3. Both these mills were equipped with the latest improvements in the industry. The giant burner in No. 3 sawmill, described as an *"Iron Bullet Waste Burner"*, was 190 feet in height, brick lined with a spark arrester on top. Mill No. 4 burner was said to be an *"Iron Bottle"* burner (probably because it was shaped like a bottle). It was 125 feet high. With mill operations vastly updated with the construction of Numbers 3 and 4, the older 1 and 2 mills gradually ceased production.

There are very few people living today who can describe the internal operation of the McLachlin Brothers sawmills. These mills, together with the company's timber and logging projects during the winter months, employed up to 1,000 men. Those who can remember the immensity of the operation do so with a nostalgic sense of loss. For those who were not here, the impact this giant industry has had upon Arnprior and the Valley is almost beyond imagination. Picture in your mind's eye some 800 men walking across the *"Mill"* bridge every morning except Sunday to commence work at seven o'clock, then returning at six p.m. after working a full ten hour shift. Yet these men were a happy and contented lot and that is the way McLachlins

meant it to be . Let your imagination wander a bit and try to create a mental image of millions of feet of choice lumber neatly piled, filling lumber yards that extended from the Ottawa River on the north, to the Canadian National Railway line on the south and east, and west to the Madawaska River. Picture the 38 miles of railway track that criss-cross this giant lumber yard.

Finally the mills, Numbers 3 and 4. The noise was deafening as the *"Twin Gates"* sliced through nine logs, stacked three in a row, much like a guillotine; forty saws one inch apart pounding up and down; the whine and growl of the *"Big Stock"*, as tons of steel chewed into the over-sized logs, echoed to the very heart of the town. In a good year McLachlins manufactured more than 60,000,000 feet of choice lumber. And that shrill whistle of Number 3 signalling the opening and shutdown of the plant each day. It has been said that with a prevailing wind, the whistle atop this sawmill could be heard at Almonte eighteen miles distant.

McLachlin Bros. No. 3 Sawmill

McLachlin Bros. No. 4 Sawmill

Photo courtesy McComb

TIMOTHY C. MULVIHILL

PERHAPS THE best and most accurate account ever written on the internal operations of the McLachlin Brothers sawmills and their ancillary operations was compiled by Timothy C. (Tim) Mulvihill for the Arnprior Chronicle many years ago. Much of this story on the mills and yard operations is derived from Mulvihill's personal experiences during the heyday of the lumbering era. Tim Mulvihill was a descendant of sturdy Irish pioneers who immigrated to Canada from Ireland in the 1850's during the potato famine, settling in Arnprior. The original Michael Mulvihill was among those who carved out with pick, shovel and dynamite, the ill-fated Chats Rapids Canal that was to bypass the rapids on the Quebec side from the tiny village of Pontiac to Union Village at the head of the Chats. The Mulvihills eventually became involved in the McLachlin enterprise with many of them serving in supervisory and trade specialist positions. Tim Mulvihill was a member of the Arnprior District High School teaching faculty for many years. An outstanding athlete, he starred with University of Toronto hockey teams and was a defensive stalwart with the famed 1927-28 Arnprior Greenshirt championship team.

The prelude to the actual lumber operation was the square timber trade. As Tim Mulvihill describes it, "*Daniel McLachlin's timber bridge across the raging Madawaska was the pinion of a vast settlement. For a hundred miles upstream the fellers, scorers and hewers harvested the 40 foot square timber destined for Quebec and the European market. From the 'Mill' Bridge to the area of the Claybank Bridge, the river was a platform of timber. Piers and sorting gaps separated McLachlin timber from that of other operators. Boom timbers guided the square timber down the river and through the 'Slide' at the 'Mill' Bridge. This 'Slide' located about centre in the bridge, carried timber over the turbulent rapids down to the calmer waters. Gates with squared timber 'stop logs', raised and lowered by chains on a windlass, controlled the flow. A government Slide Master was a permanent official and impartial judge, settling disputes between lumbermen. Every operator worked frantically to get his timber to the bridge first. Low water in late summer meant disaster for the tardy.*

"*Sawlogs were guided by booms to mills Numbers 1 and 2 for manufacture into lumber, shingles and railway ties. There were no boilers, burners or smoke stacks; the current swept the sawdust refuse downstream depositing it miles away along the south shore of Lac des Chats.*"

Wood was abundant in those days and something had to be done to dispose of the surplus. Huge slab rafts floated down river to build the "*slab dump*" forming an artificial bank on the east side of the Madawaska, in some places sixteen feet in height above the water level, from the bridge to the present Yacht Club site.

Picket Piling Ground

These white pine slabs, 14 to 18 feet long some measuring six and eight inches at the butt, were piled criss-cross along the bank. When firewood became scarce, McLachlins threw open the *"Slab Dump"* to the public. The big pine slabs were literally mined all winter and a stream of horses and sleighs crossed the ice loaded with wood.

Railway track was laid from the lumber yard across the bridge and on up Madawaska Street to Elgin to the area of Edward Street and the new railway siding. Loaded horse drawn flat cars were used and while it was quite a haul up grade, the horses just coasted back to the yard with youngsters hitching rides on the empty cars. Lumber sold for $1.00 a wagon load, all a team could haul. Houses and barns in the district were built and shingled for a few dollars. These tracks were lifted when railway sidings were constructed through the south yard to the main lines.

Nature couldn't reproduce the pine forests on the Ottawa fast enough to feed the hungry gang saws of No. 3 mill. Up two Jack Ladders the clear glistening white pine bumped end to end. Thirty million board feet, one hundred and fifty thousand logs per season was the fodder consumed by those steel monsters in that one mill. At sorting gaps timber was separated by size and species. Big burly butts were boomed for the circular saws of No. 4, producing heavy *"deal"* for export.

Up the east Jack Ladder crawled the twenty-four inch pine to drop onto a steel ramp, where a *"tailer"* with a flip of a heavy *"cantdog"* rolled it to a band saw table or hurled it to the other side where twin circulars faced it on two sides. Live rollers moved it on to the entrance of the twin gates where, if the logs were small, razor sharp teeth sliced through nine at a time; if the logs were large the dose was six.

It required just three minutes to cut six logs into one by twelve spewing out a thousand feet of choice lumber. Stripped to the waist two *"tailers"* buoyed by a fresh quid of Black Jack, slung the soggy stock to rollers before the next avalanche swamped them. On, the endless stream rolled to *"trimmers"* and *"cullers"*, then at the end of the chain *"frame loaders"* stacked the lumber high on lorries to be hauled by a single horse down the plank gangway one quarter mile to the big 325 foot long sorting table. The men who *"tailed"* the gates or loaded the *"frames"* needed no other recommendation — they had to be good.

The entire operation was not without the element of danger. Spikes embedded in the heart of a log, undetected by sorters or Jack Ladder men, shattered saws to splinters, hurling deadly steel fragments like shrapnel, with a horrifying whine. Big rough band saw logs were kicked by a steel dog that shot up from the floor on to the band saw carriage. Setters and doggers locked each securely as the carriage whizzed to the rolling band saw. Back and forth it shuttled, slicing at every trip a two inch slab. The two carriage operators manning the levers braced themselves like sailors in a high sea as the carriage whirled back and forth, with the sawyer making split second decisions as to cuts.

Up the west Jack Ladder crawled smaller logs to feed the little gates, another band saw and a re-saw. From this gate flowed the six inch to trimmers, cullers and loaders. This band saw cut off heavy slabs that moved on to the re-saw where they were sawn into desired thicknesses. From all these operations slabs and edgings rolled on chains to slash saws that reduced them to four or two foot wood. The system then emptied on to a huge trough-shaped conveyor climbing up to a belching red hot burner. Lined up on each side of this conveyor, men in leather aprons, wearing heavy mule-skin mitts, wrestled soggy slabs, piling them high on tables before picket and lath machines. On the opposite side others picked out slender slabs for wood. These were heaved into hoppers emptying into waiting carts below. Buttings or blocks had their own compartment or hopper. Short boards under six feet went for boxwood. Slabs were fed into picket machines where they were manufactured into pickets of various sizes, bundled and fastened with twine and carted off to the piling grounds. Light slabs made quarter inch lath, used as a base for plastering walls.

Above the din and turmoil, in an airy well-lighted loft overlooking the Ottawa, white-shirted filers expertly adjusted mechanical filers and gauges for the cumbersome band saws, circulars and the sturdy steel blades of the gang saws. Saws were changed at noon, at night or early morning.

Down in the belly of the dusty, greasy mill, oilers, millwrights and cleanup men crawled and crouched, oiling, adjusting or cleaning bearings and belts. The noise was ear shattering, the entire structure trembled, murderous drive shafts lurked in dark corners to fell an unwary victim. Peter Salvador, an oiler, was dragged and battered to pulp under a relentless drive shaft. A millwright was once whirled and flattened by a big belt. The slash saws always awaited a careless victim. One young fellow, just out of school, had a foot clipped off at the ankle when he slipped on a whining blade. There was tragedy, there was drudgery, there was glamor, there was challenge but there was also a feeling of security in what old-timers like to refer to as *"White Pine College"*.

THE SORTING TABLE

WHEN THE lumber reached the final stage along the conveyors it was graded by expert graders such as George St. Hilaire who could hit a horse-fly at six feet with a juicy smack of the Black Jack plug he invariably had tucked in his jaw.

Then the lumber flowed onto an electrically operated conveyor which carried the boards a quarter of a mile to the sorting table where it was sorted as to grade and length, loaded onto waiting lorries and off to the piling yards. Prior to electrification, tracks were laid the quarter mile distance and a single horse hauled small lorries loaded with lumber to the sorting stage.

THE SLIDE

THE TWO HUNDRED foot timber or log *"slide"* at the *"Mill"* Bridge was more than a conglomerate to facilitate the movement of timber down the treacherous rapids. When a log drive reached the bridge preparatory to shooting the *"slide"*, it created much excitement amongst the villagers. Buxom, calico clad matrons with babes in arms watched as the logs shot down the *"slide"* only to be caught up in the whirlpools and eddies at the foot, sometimes being hurled into the air by the force of the rapids; barefooted urchins scrambled for vantage points to watch the logs go through. Then followed the log-drivers in their battered red *"pointer"* boats, the current sucking the boats and crew into gaping jaws. The caulked booted boatsmen sealed themselves in, knees wedged against the sides, heads down, their knuckle bones showing white as they gripped the thwarts. With a swoosh, they ran the *"slide"*, then bolted over the apron to disappear momentarily in a frothy cloud. Paddles flashed as the men guided the boat from side to side dodging treacherous rocks that could rip the bottom from the cumbersome *"pointers"*.

A few courageous characters, sometimes on a bet, ran the timber *"slide"* on a forty foot stick of square timber, his only aids being a pike-pole and his caulked river boots dug tightly into the timber. The first man to go through the *"Mill"* Bridge *"slide"* was Alexander Oram, a foreman for Conroy Brothers. Oram made the remarkable ride in 1888. Shortly afterwards, the feat was performed by Arnprior's James Havey Jr. Another character of the day, *"Chain Lightning"* Stewart, is said to have gone through the *"slide"* on a stick of timber several times. In 1910, another Arnprior native, Sherman Baldwin, made the trip alone in a *"pointer"* boat. He came ashore on the west side of the river below the Roman Catholic Church, with only a little water in the boat.

In May 1912 Joseph Gaudette was appointed Government Slide Master at the *"Mill"* Bridge, with Neil McLellan as his assistant. McLellan, described as a mountain of a man, was the last Slide Master; while preparing booms in the early Spring, he slipped into the surging current and was dashed over the *"slide"* into the churning maelstrom below. Weeks later the body was dragged ashore at the Quyon boom below the Chats. The last log drive to dash over the slippery *"slide"* was pulp, logged and driven by John Findley for E. B. Eddy of Hull, in 1920.

THE PILING YARDS

THERE WAS no glamor for pilers or shippers. It was routine, heavy, steady and monotonous work. Pilers required skill and dexterity. At the age of fourteen a boy was proud when taken on piling *"shorts"*, lumber six to twelve feet long, at fifty cents a day. His only requirements were a leather apron, a hardwood whip stick and a small level. They soon learned to build bottoms, the foundations of the big lumber piles. Poorly constructed bottoms meant the piles heaved with the frost and thaws, sometimes tipping sideways or backwards. The aristocrats of the pilers were the *"Big Stock"* men. They handled the 1 x 12, 2 x 12 and 4 x 12. They used hooks with three foot handles to draw the planks into place. Extreme care had to be taken so that no mark was left on this lumber. It was for export market. These piles were low built and covered immediately to prevent checking.

Photo courtesy Ontario Archives and E. P. Hall

McLachlin Bros. Piling Yards

Water Mills and Slide, Arnprior, Canada.

Photo courtesy Peg Whyte

Water Mills and Slide, 1907

Photo courtesy Jean Macnamara Cunningham

The Shippers

THE WOOD PILERS

THERE WERE thousands of cords of wood, twenty inch, four foot and buttings, piled in the McLachlin lumber yards each summer. The job was under contract to Louis Lapierre and he made it a family affair. Louis and his five boys, Edgar, Liguori, Tommy, Antonio (Tony) and Ferdinand (Fergie), did the job and kept the wagons and dump carts busy six days a week from the late April opening until the mill closed in October. The wood was stock piled and later sold at minimum rates to townspeople. The Lapierre lads were a jolly crew of French Canadians, often singing while they worked. During the height of its popularity, Edgar enjoyed singing *"I'm Looking Over a Four Leaf Clover"*. Louis was a relatively small man but the boys knew who was the boss. Liguori recalls piling wood in the McLachlin yards at the age of ten years.

THE SHIPPERS

SHIPPERS HAD no easy time of it. The scaler was boss of six men and a tally boy. A box car was spotted before piles to be loaded. A smooth hardwood bar with a screw attachment was fastened firmly across the centre of the door. Two men packed in the car, the other four fed the lumber over the bar. The drone of the scaler never ceased calling the measurements of every board and the tally boy repeated them monotonously after him as he ticked off his tally card.

One of Arnprior's fine characters, N. Alan Campbell, tells this story of his days with McLachlins.

"Everyone worked in McLachlins in those days — there was no other place to work. I was hired by John Mulvihill in 1920 and was acquainted with the General Superintendent Armon Burwash. I was paid about two dollars a day and all I did was put in ice at Burwash's residence — the ice man brought the ice — I took out the old ice, washed the sawdust from the new blocks and replaced it in the ice box." Continuing, Alan said, *"That's all I had to do except hide for the rest of the day, sometimes hanging around the machine shop until Ollie Murphy kicked me out — then I would swim across the Madawaska and on to the wharf until the kids told on me."* Eventually Campbell got to be a measurer in the mill with Joseph Dussiaume a culler-grader. He also subbed as a measurer and tally boy in the yard and tells an amusing story of his final episode with the lumber firm. Alan says it happened this way: *"I was out to a dance the night before and the next day I was sent to the yard to measure for 'Long Billy' Mulvihill".* The measurements of the lumber would be called out by Mulvihill and Alan's job was to jot down the figures. Said Alan, *"I sat in the shade between the lumber piles, fell asleep and was rudely awakened when Mulvihill called in a loud voice, 'how much is in the car?'"* Mulvihill knew it was near the required ten thousand feet. *"Without replying,"* Campbell said, *"I sneaked away, went home but did not tell my father."* Shortly thereafter Alan's dad met John

Mulvihill and queried, *"How's the young lad doing?"* Mulvihill replied, *"I fired him last week."*

BIG CAR MEN AND BIG CAR HORSES

MANY YEARS ago in a locality between what is now Second and Third Avenues, stood an open weather-beaten drive shed. The open end faced south. This was home base for six teams of *"big car"* horses and their teamsters referred to as *"big car"* men.

Here they rested between trips or took shelter from blinding snow storms that swept down from the Laurentians across Chats Lake to bury two hundred acres of lumber piles and miles of track and in the blazing heat of July, when violent thunderstorms cracked and sizzled along the curcuitous network of railway tracks, teamsters were cautioned to leave their perilous perches on the steel bumpers of the box cars and take shelter.

These men and horses were the elite of the industry. Six mammoth teams, each animal weighing one ton or more, moved the harvest of the biggest lumber operation of the period to the railway siding. The teamsters were selected by the Yard Superintendent and Barn Boss. They were quiet family men with an inordinate love and understanding of their charges. No horse had ever been injured or mistreated in their hands and the veterinarian, George Styles, with a watchful eye, ensured good care of the horses. McLachlins never would tolerate the abuse of any animal and a teamster who tended towards such treatment lost his job immediately. At six o'clock each morning they were at the stables, grooming the horses and preparing for the day. When they returned in the evening, the teamsters remained to hose down the horse's foam stained coats and they often returned on Sunday to clip fetlocks and trim shaggy manes. Their horse's weight, digestion, sleekness of hide and food consumption were under constant scrutiny. The *"Big Car"* man's pay envelope contained more money. *"Big Car"* horses as well as men were screened. The breeder who sold a team of Clydesdales, Percherons or Belgians for work on the big cars often were paid five to six hundred dollars, a lot of money in those days. The owner's bragging was discounted.

The scales had to tip 2000 pounds or more and the horse's temperament had to match the drivers. The Barn Boss who purchased these leviathans was never deceived by appearances or puffing by salesmen. He listened politely and made an appointment for the man to demonstrate his wares. When a deal was arranged, every teamster, piler, lorryman and water boy knew of the arrangement.

"The rangy, grizzled farmer in the faded blue bibbed overalls, smiled confidently as he led his team of dapple greys to the Big Crossing. A loaded box car hove into sight, the brakeman on top, the teamster straddling the coupler with tight reins. The foreman flagged down the team. What thoughts ran riot in that old man's mind as he deftly swung the greys about and helped hitch them to the heavily loaded car. He knew his horses and he needed the money they would fetch but they had never been trained to lug or start

dead weights like loaded box cars. Gently he eased the collars, freed the trapped manes and patted the glossy flanks before picking up the reins. The mares showed no tension. The old man was at their heels. He leaned slightly back to tighten the lines. The on-lookers were hushed. The broad Percherons leaned into the collars feeling the load; the traces rose; the whiffle trees sighed; the back pads sprung off the sleek round backs; dust spurted under the curved straining legs. The nigh mare stepped over the rail; the old man pulled them up with a 'whoa girls'. Slowly he reached for the straps and again leaned gently back. The sparks and dust flew; a slight creak; the wheels moved; the old man gasped, 'Doll, Queen,' and the stubborn car groaned into motion. A joyous roar erupted from that motley fascinated group of spectators. The horses had proven themselves; the deal was made and the old man went home with mixed feelings. He had the money but he felt the loss of his trusted horses."

Spring was a joyous season on the banks of the Madawaska. The shreik of the *"Mill"* whistle brought contentment to the hearts of the townspeople. The cattle were at pasture, the gardens were burgeoning; the men-folk all had work. The raging river was in spate hurling lofty plumes and mist high above the timber *"slide"*. John Murphy was out early that morning. It was not yet seven; but a car had to be spotted for an early freight train. The fragrance of the young morning was not lost on John as he straddled the iron bumper. The siding was between the two railroad bridges; the track crossed highway 17 east of the present bridge. A low gate, with one sturdy bar was always closed at night to keep out errant cows. John was crossing the road. The horses danced gaily on. Suddenly the huge

team reared, swung sideways tangled in the wire fence; John was hurled from his perch. Both legs were mangled and had to be amputated. The gate had not been opened and apparently the horses panicked. For years, a stout, dark moustachioed man in a wheel chair crossed the *"Mill"* Bridge daily. John Murphy had learned to make harness for the *"Big Car"* horses.

THE DINKY ENGINE

IN TIME progress replaced the *"Big Car"* horses. A diesel locomotive known as the *"Dinky"* engine, was designed by Engineer Johnson and built to specifications at the John Inglis Toronto plant about 1912, taking over the task of moving the big lumber laden railway cars throughout the McLachlin lumber yards. Kids marvelled at the tiny locomotive and tried to hitch rides on it.

Benny Frieday, with a twinkle in his eye, recalls engineers Lloyd Cartwright and Jack Thoms peppering the kids with water which they had loaded in a grease gun, a harmless method to discourage them.

THE HARNESS SHOP

THE McLACHLIN Harness Shop, in which all harness and equipment for the hundreds of horses in the McLachlin stables was made, was under the jurisdiction of the genial Dave McComb, a man who never hesitated to stitch the leather cover on a baseball and patch up baseball gloves for the kids who frequently came to him for help. And *"gum rubbers"* or *"oil tan"*, mocassins were a cold thing unless one had a thick felt insole in them and McComb often provided these for the children as well; all without charge.

Photo courtesy Ontario Archives

The Dinky Engine

BLACKSMITH SHOP AND WAGON SHOP

THE BLACKSMITH Shop, another very busy unit in the lumbering business, was in charge of Bill Bullard.

Among the first foremen in McLachlins Wagon Shop was James Nicholson. After Nicholson's death McLachlins requested Andrew Fulton to take charge. Among those who worked in the Wagon Shop were Fred Shaw and Joseph Desormia. This was an exceptionally busy branch of the lumbering complex. Scores of wagons, dump carts and sleighs had to be built and maintained. The McLachlin *"pointer"* boats were also built in the Wagon Shop.

THE SAWDUST EXPRESS

THE OTTAWA Exhibition was just as popular, probably more so, than it is today, back in the booming lumbering era of Arnprior. McLachlins, recognizing what this meant to their employees and their families, made arrangements each year with the Canadian Pacific Railway to operate a special train from Arnprior to Ottawa, returning the same evening.

Both mills, all yard and ancillary operations would cease for that day and most everyone, along with their families, would board the ten car *"sawdust special"* train and off to the Fair. McLachlin paid the entire bill including midway rides, ice-cream and all the things kids love.

FIRE PROTECTION

FIRE PROTECTION in the mills and vast lumber yards was, of course, of prime importance. Certain requirements issued by the insurance people had to be adhered to. Prior to the establishing of an electric plant in sawmill No. 1, oil lamps and lanterns were the only means of light. Heat was generated by stoves and hot water. Fuel in the mills was sawdust and refuse. Eventually McLachlins converted a section of the water-powered mill No. 1 to provide electricity for their use. Water mains from this private system were not available in winter. It was not until after the municipal waterworks system was constructed that the lumber firm had a water supply for all seasons. An eight inch pipe was installed beneath the Madawaska River up stream from the bridge and connected to the town supply. The turbine used in providing the first electric power in Arnprior was reclaimed from the Madawaska River when the present new bridge and weir were built through the initiative of Edgar H. Burwash who suggested to the then Mayor, George Johnson, that the turbine be preserved for history. It now lies in the vicinity of the new filtration plant. By 1905 fire protection in the McLachlin Brother mills and yards consisted of the following: 950 feet of hose in No. 3 mill; 450 feet in No. 4; 1350 feet in the east and west yards; 350 feet in the south yard; and 750 feet was kept on four reels in reserve. There were 65 pails of water in No. 2 mill; 75 pails in No. 3; and 52 pails in No. 4. Barrels of water were scattered throughout the lumber yards. Of course, there was no smoking allowed other than at designated stations. In those early days townspeople pastured their cows in the lumber yards and each morning and evening scores of cattle were herded over the bridge to pasture. In addition to providing choice feed for the animals, the grazing kept the grass low thus minimizing the danger of fire. Then there was an elaborate sprinkler system operating from a concrete building in which were housed numerous control valves that operated the apparatus protecting No. 3 sawmill. The sprinkler building was located on the property presently owned by Reg and Shirley Wagenblass.

McLACHLIN BUILT RESIDENCES

THE McLACHLIN family constructed several fine homes in Arnprior, most of which are still in existence, classed among the finer dwellings in the town and of historical significance to Arnprior.

THE HILL

The stone mansion on the high bluff overlooking the Ottawa River known originally as *"The Hill"* and mentioned frequently throughout this narrative, was built by the first Daniel McLachlin in 1853. Subsequent McLachlin families resided there until it was sold in 1933 to R. M. Gemmel. As mentioned previously, *"The Hill"* was purchased finally by the Oblate Order of Mary Immaculate and is now known as *"Galilee Community"*. The approach to *"The Hill"* was, and still is, beautiful. The original *"Gate"* and *"Coachman's"* house at the fork in the road separating the lakeside approach to the front entrance, and the road used most generally, to the rear of the residence, is in excellent condition. Another residential house situated midway between the *"Gate"* house and the main residence along this road, has been completely renovated and is occupied by the Sisters of St. Martha who are working at Galilee.

The outbuildings are in fair condition. In one of these was located the private school where the McLachlin children were tutored by Professor Hedley Bridge who was lured from Ashbury College to Arnprior for this purpose. After the private school ceased to exist, Bridge went to work in the McLachlin office.

THE ORIGINAL CONVENT

Situated on the block where the present homes of Dominic and Mort Sullivan are located, was another large frame residence also built by the original Daniel McLachlin. It was purchased in 1894 by Rev. J. A. M. Chaine, Parish Priest of St. John Chrysostom Church, for use as a residence for the Sisters of Charity of Halifax, who came to Arnprior as teaching Sisters in the local school. The building was subsequently used solely as a school, supplementing the brick St. John Chrysostom school on Albert Street. It was later sold and demolished following the opening of the new St. Joseph's school in January 1951.

SACRED HEART CONVENT

In time Father Chaine arranged for the purchase of the expansive Victorian style brick dwelling just across John Street from the old Convent, for use as the new Convent presently occupied by the Sisters of Providence of St. Vincent de Paul who arrived in Arnprior from Kingston in 1909. This home was built by Claude McLachlin.

DR. R. W. LANG RESIDENCE

The large brick home on the corner of Church and John Streets, presently owned by Dr. R. W. and Mrs. Lang, was built by Hugh F. McLachlin for his widowed mother Mrs. Daniel McLachlin. This luxurious residence was owned and lived in for many years by the deRenzy family.

EDGEWOOD

Many will remember the large English style frame residence and spacious grounds at the northeast corner of John Street fronting the Ottawa River. The property owned by the first Daniel McLachlin, was acquired by Jack Usborne a descendant of the Usborne lumber people of Portage du Fort, who married Jessie McLachlin, daughter of the first Daniel and Mrs. McLachlin. Usborne built *"Edgewood"* and resided there for many years. The entire area, presently park land, was developed to such an extent that it was known province-wide as a vineyard and apple orchard of note, not to mention the spacious flower gardens throughout. In addition to the *"Edgewood"* property, Jack Usborne was in charge of the Waba vineyard for the Renfrew Fruit and Floral Company for some years. Usborne describes his experimental work with apples and grapes in an Ontario Agricultural Commission report of 1881. The Waba vineyard consisted of one hundred acres of land lying between the Waba Creek, the Madawaska River and the second line of Fitzroy. It was managed for Usborne for ten years by John Cooney, father of Percival J. Cooney, author of *"Kinsmen"* and later a teaching professor and Director of Americanization in the El Monte, California University. Another son, Frank, who once worked in the grocery store of E. C. Armand on John Street, became a large grocery wholesaler in Montana and was elected Governor of the State of Montana. The Cooney family left Arnprior for the United States in 1891.

Eventually Jack Usborne sold *"Edgewood"* to Claude McLachlin who, as previously mentioned, was the grandfather of Norma and Pat Hall. The stately residence became the summer home for Mr. and Mrs. S. D. Hall and their family for many years.

MACNAMARA RESIDENCE

The distinguished white board and batten home on Daniel Street at the approach to the bridge, owned by Jean Macnamara Cunningham, was also built by H. F. McLachlin who occupied it until he moved to *"The Hill"* after his father's death. Among the fine heritage homes in Arnprior, it has been lived in continuously by the Macnamara family since Richard Macnamara came to Arnprior from Quebec City at the request of H. F. McLachlin, to manage the McLachlin Brothers office.

There was also a large frame dwelling just east of the McLachlin office which was lived in for a time by John H. Burwash, Vice-President of the McLachlin firm.

RESIDENCE OF THE LAST DANIEL, LOMBARDY PLACE

The large brick building on John Street presently the Arnprior & District Memorial Hospital, was built by the last Daniel McLachlin as his personal home. Prior to this the family lived in the house next to the brick office.

STEAMBOATS ON LAC DES CHATS

THE MEN WHO pioneered the forwarding trade on the Upper Ottawa River had many serious obstacles to overcome before they were able to ensure safe and expeditious movement of passengers and freight between Bytown and Portage du Fort. They were obliged to risk their wood-burning steamers upon waters unchartered and which were notorious for the perplexing and tortuous channels, treacherous eddies and currents which existed sometimes in proximity to waterfalls. There was no pilot whose knowledge of the route was sufficiently wide to guide steamers with safety and until the pioneer navigators themselves undertook the work of charting the lakes they were in imminent danger of running their craft upon hidden shoals. That such disaster did not occur more frequently, than proved to be the case, was providential.

There were no wharves or portage roads to facilitate the movement of freight and long delays enroute were necessary in order that passengers might be put ashore by small boats. The very continuance of their operations was also a matter of uncertainty, for their traffic was almost entirely dependent upon the extent of the lumbering operations and the establishment of settlers. The towing of logs was not adopted until some years afterwards.

Chats Lake with its submerged reefs and numerous shoals was a particularly hazardous stretch of water, 21 miles from the Chats Rapids to the Chenaux. For a time, raft pilots were engaged with varying success. Finally Captain William Richards decided to make a detailed examination of the lake by means of a small boat. Every spare hour was devoted to this survey. Soundings were made and charts were set up, upon which were entered the depth of the water, the islands, distinguishing landmarks, shoals, etc. When this was completed the *"George Buchanan"* was sailed down the channel by compass, the course and time lapsed duly noted. This was with a view to facilitating and safeguarding navigation in time of possible fog. The channel so designed has been used continuously to the present day.

There were four passenger boats, all wood-burning, plying Chats Lake at various intervals. The first was the *"George Buchanan"* built in Arnprior in 1836 by Captain William Grant, to the order of Buchanan, Simpson and Mittleberger. This boat (previously described) was also under the command, for a time, of Captain William Richards with Captain D. K. Cowley as steward.

The second passenger boat, the "Oregon" (also previously described) was built in Montreal by the Molson people and shipped in sections to Hubbell's Falls (Galetta) where it was assembled at "Steen's Landing". The "Oregon" was under the command of Captain D. K. Cowley and a Captain Loney.

The Union Forwarding Company built the steamer "Alliance" in 1865 at Sand Point. The commander was a Captain G. Brown.

The fourth steamboat built for passenger service was the "Prince Arthur". Described as "the finest, most powerful and fastest boat ever upon the lake" the "Prince Arthur" was built in 1870 at Sand Point. It was destroyed by fire at Portage du Fort.

There was keen competition amongst those four boats, most often with minimal success and at times with serious damage to the boats, all anxious to assume their superiority over the Chenaux Rapids up to Portage du Fort during the peak Spring flood.

The "Alliance" was eventually replaced by the "J. L. Murphy" about 1885, with Captain J. Picard in command. The Union Forwarding people also operated the steamer "Baldwin" on Chats Lake under the command of Captain Philip Toner. This boat was replaced by the "Perley" with the same engines and a new boiler and with Toner in Command. The "Perley" burned in 1895 and was replaced by the "Hamilton". After many years of service the "Hamilton" was sunk in a deep channel at the foot of the Chenaux.

About 1889 a small ferry boat owned and operated by Captain D. K. Cowley, named the "Janet Craig" plied between Sand Point and Bristol. A small bay on the Quebec side of the river opposite Gillies Brothers sawmill, known by old-timers as the "ferry landing", was probably the Quebec dock for this boat. A road commonly referred to as the "ferry road" cut through the dense bush from the "landing" to Bristol. There still remains evidence of this road and timber bridges over creeks and gullies.

After the towing operations were taken over by the Upper Ottawa Improvement Company in 1865, the alligator "Samson" was put into service on Chats Lake. Gillies Brothers, in 1923, built the steel boat "William Douglas". The Gillies people later constructed the steel-plated, diesel-powered "White Bear" which saw service at Temagami and Braeside.

In 1910 the "Hiram Robinson" was built and the "J. L. Murphy" dismantled and sunk at the head of the Chats. Next to the McLachlin boats, the "Robinson" was perhaps the most familiar to the people of Arnprior. It often tied up at the town wharf and youngsters delighted in diving from its upper decks. The "Hiram Robinson" also went to a watery grave at the head of the Chats Rapids.

THE McLACHLIN FLEET

THE FIRST McLachlin steamboat on Lac des Chats was the "Pontiac", built in 1890. The McLachlin firm also had three "alligators", the "Amable du Fond", the "Bonnechere" and the "Madawaska". These were flat-bottom, steel constructed side-wheelers that could be hauled over land by means of a winch.

The steamer "Pontiac" burned in July 1908 and construction was commenced immediately on a new and much bigger flagship which was eventually christened the "Opeongo". The hull was of two-inch oak plank and steel-plated. A side-wheeler, the "Opeongo" was about 100 feet in length with a beam of 40 feet. It boasted a crew of six, plus a cook and it contained a spacious dining room.

The "Opeongo" was ceremoniously launched April 29, 1909 at the launchways on the east bank of the Madawaska at its confluence with the Ottawa. That widely known character, George Johnson, chief engineer for McLachlin Brothers, who built the Queen of the fleet, was in charge of proceedings. The entire town was represented, including clergymen and civic officials. A special cable was in place to prevent the boat from striking on a particularly rocky side; at a given time the cable was to be cut through by a man in readiness with an axe. The "ways" were greased, the chocks pulled but for some reason the fellow with the axe was slow; Johnson, who was noted for a flippant tongue, forgot or didn't worry about the dignitaries, and hollered in a booming voice, "cut that damn cable". The boat slid down the "ways" without incident. One of the Captains on the "Opeongo" was Leo Tanguay. After the shutdown of the McLachlin operation the "Opeongo" was stripped to its hull, loaded with rock and steel rails and sunk in 45 feet of water at the mouth of the Madawaska.

In 1905 the McLachlin firm had built the tug-boat "Donald McDonald", named after a pioneer McLachlin employee. A side-wheeler, the boat was 50 feet long with a beam of about 16 feet and a draught of four feet. One of the Captains of the "McDonald" was Clifton "Kip" Cotie. The towman on this boat was Ferdinand Lapierre. It had a crew of four men. After the close of operations the "Donald McDonald" was sold and operated on the Gatineau River.

A second tug-boat, the "Jean Macnamara", was built about 1918. There is a human interest story connected with the naming of the "Jean Macnamara"

When the boat was built, Dan McLachlin suggested to Richard Macnamara, Secretary-Treasurer of the company, that the new boat be named after Macnamara's wife. However, Mrs. Macnamara refused the honor and suggested the boat be named after her granddaughter, 12-year-old Jean Macnamara and this was accepted by McLachlin. This created quite a hub-bub at the school when it was learned the boat was being christened after the 12-year-old. Some could not believe it and one fellow Alan Boyce, walked the two miles to the "boom" camp to confirm it. The "Jean", as it was commonly referred to, was about 50 feet in length, with a beam of 16 feet. It carried a four man crew, had a steel hull and was equipped with stabilizers to prevent roll. It was captained at different times by Jack Moffatt and Joe Deschenes with "Kip" Cotie and Eugene Lacombe as crew members. When the shut-down occurred, the boat was sold for salvage.

Lacombe actually captained the *"Jean Macnamara"* for a short time at the age of 17. He also worked as towman and did a stint of firing the boiler on this boat. Chuckling away, Lacombe tells of an incident long ago when the flagship *"Opeongo"* had sounded the whistle signal for the *"Jean"* to go out and pick up a big boom of logs which the *"Opeongo"* had towed from the Chenaux Rapids. For some reason, George L. Graham, McLachlin chief timber limit agent, was called to the wharf at the *"boom"* camp, just as the *"Jean"* was steaming up for the run out in the lake. With Captain Joe Deschenes at the wheel, Lacombe poured the coal to the boiler; a cloud of smoke and ink-black soot poured from the stack just as Graham reached boatside. It might have been alright with the usually calm Graham but it was Sunday and he was all dressed up for church, replete with starched white shirt. The jet black smoke and soot converted the white shirt into a black polka dot one. Lacombe said, *"I never heard Graham curse before but he sure cursed that time."*

There have been several ferry boats on Chats Lake but none with the prominence of the 72 foot steel-hulled craft, the *"Norvic-Ottawa"*. Built in 1922 in Montreal by Vicker's Marine, the boat derived its name from its home harbor, Norway Bay and its builders, Vickers. It was used primarily in ferry service carrying passengers, cars and freight to and from Sand Point and Norway Bay, a journey of three miles across the Ottawa River. The boat was commissioned and put into service in 1923. Old-timers at the Norway Bay summer resort area, as well as people residing in the riverside communities of Sand Point, Braeside and Arnprior, remember fondly the early 1930's when the *"Norvic"* was the scene of many moonlight cruises on Chats Lake. The *"Norvic"* had, for all intents and purposes, outlived its usefulness in 1962. After removal of the engine and useable parts, the boat was abandoned and beached at Chenaux Rapids. Among the Commanders in charge of the *"Norvic"* were Captains Chartier and Flemming. Chartier always wore a full uniform with captain's hat complete with gold braid. The *"Norvic"* bell is now tolling in the belfry of the non-denominational church at Norway Bay. A few years ago the boat was raised, pumped out and towed twenty-one miles down Chats Lake to Vydon Acres where it was loaded on transport floats and taken to the Manotick marina where some thought was being given to renovation.

The *"Norway Belle"* was another steamboat ferrying passengers on the lake prior to the *"Norvic"*.

There are hundreds of small boats now plying the waters of Lac des Chats but the era of the big steamboats is gone forever.

McLachlin Bros. fleet. Left to right: Jean Macnamara, Donald McDonald and Opeongo

TIMBER RAFTING ON THE OTTAWA

THERE IS A plaque near the mouth of the Madawaska River commemorating the era of timber rafting on the Ottawa River. While it does not mention the hardy pioneer rivermen who lived and worked on these rafts all the way through to Quebec City, surely anyone reading of this will recall the people who opened up the entire Ottawa Valley for future generations. The plaque, erected by the Archaeological and Historic Sites' Board of Ontario, reads as follows:

"The rafting of square timber down the Ottawa River begun in 1806 reached its peak during 1861-91 and ended in 1909. Pine sticks from one to two feet square and 40 to 50 feet long were floated down tributary rivers such as the Petawawa, Madawaska, Bonnechere and Mississippi to rafting points on the Ottawa. There, cribs were made up containing 20 to 40 pieces of timber and as many as 200 cribs were in turn assembled into a raft. These rafts could be taken apart for passage down rapids or the timber slides which by-passed them. Arriving at Quebec City as much as two months later, they were dismantled and the timber loaded for shipment overseas."

The transport ships awaiting the timber, had huge bulkheads in the bow of the vessels where the timber was loaded on board.

THE BRIDGES

THE BUCHANAN brothers must have chosen the proper location for the initial bridge to span the Madawaska River. For it is in the exact location that subsequent structures have been erected including the present new four-lane bridge opened for traffic on July 13, 1976.

The bridge most referred to in this story is the *"Mill"* Bridge but there were others in existence at one time or another as well. This *"Mill"* Bridge was the private property of the McLachlin's though the public used it at will. As more roads were opened and traffic increased, a second timber structure was built several hundred yards upstream from the *"Mill"* Bridge. This was of two spans. It was carried by two piers, timber and stone filled, with a deck of heavy plank. It served for many years but time took its toll and it is said to have collapsed under the weight of a threshing mill. Then a new bridge of steel was built. This was known as the *"Iron"* bridge. It was finally demolished and sold for scrap. The *"Iron"* Bridge was located a few hundred yards above the present structure and connected with Elgin Street. Following the rupture in the timbered *"Mill"* Bridge on Easter Sunday, 1927, a concrete replacement was built. This was in turn replaced with the present four-lane structure.

One of the last Timber Cribs descending Chats 1909

Photo courtesy Arnprior Museum, Hanson, Lavoie collection

Original timber bridge. Mill No. 2 at left.

First concrete bridge

THE McLACHLIN OFFICE

IN COMPARISON with modern day offices, the two-storey brick McLachlin Brothers office situated at the southeast extremity of the *"Mill"* Bridge, was relatively very small. But millions of dollars were disbursed from the tiny building to thousands of mill workers and shantymen down through the years. For a period of seven years the only girl employed in the McLachlin office was Mae Frizell, a Carleton Place native, who was Secretary and general *"office girl"* of the day.

Mae Frizell, now Mrs. Norman McLachlin, recalls her years within the financial walls of the lumber dynasty. Also employed in the office in an accounting capacity was Norman McLachlin, a cousin of the lumber people and the man she eventually married. The courtship was not an instant thing; Norman apparently was making up his mind very carefully. Mae says, *"I never looked at him but he must have been looking at me,"* and he finally broke the ice and they began dating. They were married July 10, 1929.

Mrs. McLachlin worked in the same office with Charles Macnamara, the Secretary-Treasurer of the company, whom she says *"was the nicest man to work for, a real gentleman".* With a smile she recalls the frequent visits to the office by George Johnson, the eccentric chief engineer, with business items scribbled down on bits of paper. Looking at the stuff, Macnamara would comment, *"Oh, the man on the galloping horse."* Some other office employees recalled by Mrs. McLachlin include John H. Burwash, Vice-President; M. D. Graham, Hedley Bridge, Harry Newham, Webster McCallum, J. S. Simpson, Godfrey Burwash and Jim McManus.

George Johnson was one of the many characters within the McLachlin enterprise. Born in Campbellton, N.B., he saw service in the South African war. On return to Canada

McLachlin Office 1903

Photo courtesy Ontario Archives, C. Macnamara collection

New 4 lane bridge

Photo courtesy Hanson

he was associated with McGill University in Montreal as a demonstrating engineer, remaining there until McLachlin Brothers secured his services as chief engineer on January 1, 1904. During the First Great War, Johnson had a distinguished record and was awarded the Legion of Honor by France, and the Order of the British Empire by the British government. He died suddenly in Arnprior at age 55.

Many of the so-called engineers that operated the giant engines in the McLachlin complex could not read or write, although they were outstanding in their specific positions. In some way Johnson obtained the required licenses for them. Typical of Johnson was a quip referring to the loyalty of the McLachlin staff when he said: *"I can find 12 men among the McLachlin employees more dependable than the 12 Apostles."* Another Johnson story: While in France during World War 1 he had a particular assignment requiring him to work during the night. He was on the outskirts of a city and decided he should take a lunch along. Passing a street-corner lunch counter he said to the girl attendant: *"I'd like a couple of hard-boiled eggs to take out."* The waitress smiled blandly, sidled up and said, *"O.K., but you'll have to wait, me and Mamie don't get off until ten."*

THE "BOOM CAMP" AND McLACHLIN HOUSE BOATS

ALL THE youngsters who carried lunch to their dads working anywhere in the McLachlin complex knew all about the *"boom"* camp and the huge plates of beans and chunks of home-made pie to which they were quite frequently treated by good-natured chefs such as Tom Dore. And the pies were big ones and cut in just four pieces; the beans, all a kid could eat.

The *"boom"* camp was a big two-storey building, located on the high bluff about 300 yards east of No. 4 mill. The upper flat provided sleeping quarters for the boat and boom crews who were more or less on 24 hour duty, always in readiness to answer the whistle call from the *"Opeongo"* or the *"Robinson"* to pick up a large tow of logs in mid-lake. Because of numerous shoals, the big steamboats had to remain in the deep channel waters and would signal for the tug-boats to come pick up the tow. Johnny Groves and George Graham were the last two supervisors in charge of the *"boom"* camp. The *"boom"* camp crew acted as unofficial firemen for any shore fires east as far as the Chats Rapids.

McLachlins also had two house-boats, the *"Chaperone"* and the *"Flirt"*, which were towed to a sheltered bay somewhere on the lake where picnics were held. They also had a large covered horse-drawn picnic wagon in which the family and guests were taken on outings.

And what was probably the first golf course in the immediate area, McLachlins had a 5-hole course just west of *"The Hill"* residence. This was in the early 1900's.

DECLINE

ALTHOUGH NO ONE wanted to believe it, there were signs of pending decline in the early 1920's of the once fabulous McLachlin lumbering empire. Hugh F. McLachlin, whose benevolence towards those in need made him much loved by the employees, and his younger brother Claude, also well respected, both inheriting the beneficent mannerisms of their father, were outstanding lumbermen and the enterprise was in good hands. But extenuating circumstances seemed to increase as the years went by. Although younger, Claude died April 19, 1904, at the age of 50 years. Hugh F. passed away September 13, 1912 at 69 years of age. The Presidency then went to Daniel, the last Dan.

The so-called *"ten lost years"* of the great depression were fast approaching; the lumber market was in decline; the McLachlin timber limits were almost cut out but there still remained some hope.

There was plenty of pulp available on the limits and during the depression years that followed immediately after the sawmills ceased operation in 1929, Dan McLachlin said his company had considered the erection of a mechanical pulp plant, the cost of which was half a million dollars but he was apprehensive of such an expenditure with economic conditions as they were at the time. McLachlin said his limits contained sufficient pulpwood to keep a one hundred ton mechanical pulp mill going almost indefinitely. There still remained a flicker of light. In 1934 McLachlin contracted to saw logs for J. R. Booth Company and No. 3 operated for five months. There was a rumor that Booth was interested in acquiring the mills, grounds and limits but again the overall cost of renovation may have negated the transaction.

The final gasp of the great McLachlin Brothers lumber odyssey came October 27, 1934 when engineers at No. 3 sawmill, the biggest ever in the era of the McLachlin empire, cut the power and let the giant engines wind down never again to reopen.

The mansion on *"The Hill"* was sold to R. M. Gemmel in 1933. Gemmel renovated the residence and renamed it *"Raithmuir"* but to old Ottawa Valley people it always remained *"The Hill"*. It was later purchased by Colonel W. H. Hadley, who in turn sold it to the Oblate Order of Mary Immaculate in 1946 who now operate the stately home as a Novitiate for boys preparing for the priesthood and as a renewal and retreat centre. This last ownership seems to take on a sort of transcendental significance that one likes to believe would be favored by the original builder the first Daniel McLachlin.

McLachlin Boom Camp

Logs on Madawaska 1899

THE LAST DANIEL McLACHLIN

A FORLORN, LONELY man, walked up John Street every day and out across the bridge to the little brick office once the power hall where many big decisions were made. He was the last Daniel McLachlin. It is perhaps fitting that the last President of the McLachlin firm was also Daniel, referred to as the last Dan, a son of Hugh F. He, like his predecessors, maintained excellent rapport with employees. Highly respected by the townspeople, he served for years on Town Council and as Mayor of Arnprior. The man loved people and enjoyed talking with anyone who dropped by. On one occasion as he sat with pipe in mouth, feet propped up on his desk, talking with a newspaper reporter, he said: *"This place is 10 percent business office and 90 percent smoking room."* His princely residence on John Street is now the Arnprior and District Memorial Hospital and the story is told that after he had been approached about selling the home for hospital utilization he walked into the Town Hall one day and handed the keys of the residence to the Town Clerk. Regardless of what the circumstances might have been, this gesture is typical of the entire McLachlin family. The last Dan was born in 1881 and died in 1954. And so perhaps the greatest epoch ever to be in the history of Arnprior came to an end.

ARNPRIOR AND DISTRICT HISTORICAL SOCIETY

M AY 1978 was an important period with respect to Arnprior because at that time the preservation of our heritage took a giant step when the Arnprior and District Historical Society came into being. It is also significant to note that the first President was not among the seniors of Arnprior but rather an 18 year old Arnprior District High School student, Philip Powell, son of Marjorie and Harry Powell lifelong Arnprior residents. Powell was the youngest President of any Historical Society in Canada at the time and a plaque commemorating this was presented to him by the local Historical group. Powell and Carol Ann Cuthbert were honored at a dinner in appreciation of their work in the interest of Arnprior's heritage. The Secretary at the time was Gale Larsen.

The current Executive of the Society is composed of: President, Janet Clancy; Past President, Ernest B. Wolff; Vice-President, Edna Carey; Secretary, Janet Carmichael; Treasurer, Mabel Simpson; Program Committee, Gerry White, Miriam McCreary, Marion Needham.

Other Presidents were: 1979, Heather Lang Runtz; 1980, E. B. Wolff; 1981-1982-1983-1984, Janet Clancy. The office of Secretary since 1979 has been filled by Janet Carmichael.

In 1978 the Eastern Ontario Historical Conference was held in Arnprior. Of particular interest is the fact that it is said this is the first occasion that the Conference has been held in a small community.

The Society went all out in its fight to save the Canadian Pacific Railway station from demolition and also battled to prevent the razing of the walls of the heritage stone structure on the west bank of the Madawaska River, a large building erected in the early era of McLachlin Brothers, which served in many capacities down through the years. However both ventures proved unsuccessful.

Since its founding back in 1978, the Arnprior and District Historical Society has been extremely active. Noted speakers have addressed the membership on matters ranging from the heyday of the Opeongo Road, the Horse Railway, the Royal Visit in 1860 and the lumbering era back to its infancy and up to the present day.

THE FIRST TELEPHONE AND TELEGRAPH

T HE FIRST telephones were installed in Arnprior in August 1887 when fourteen subscribers were listed. No telephone numbers were used. A notice was prominently displayed on pages of the telephone directory which contained the names of all telephone users in Eastern Ontario and Quebec which merely states: *The name of the party wanted should be spoken with special distinctness to prevent mistakes."* Another notation said: *"Do not attempt to use the telephone on the approach of or during a thunderstorm."*

The first telephone subscribers in Arnprior were: The Bank of Ottawa; Canadian Pacific Railway Station; A. J. Campbell, Merchant; Doctor J. G. Cranston; R. D. Fetherston, Agent; D. M. Finnie, Bank of Ottawa; Michael Galvin, Merchant; J. B. Lyon, Hotel; Alex Menzies, Drugs; Alex Menzies residence; McLachlin Brothers Office; Claude McLachlin; A. McPhee, Hotel; and B. V. Stafford.

It was October 1886 that the Canadian Pacific Telegraph wires were installed in Arnprior. The telegraph office was in the office of the Chronicle and the telegraph operator was Henry Needham.

CHARACTERS — PAST AND PRESENT

E ACH GENERATION has its *"characters"*, a sort of combination of historian, story teller, a relater of anecdotes. These people are really a part of a community's history, a people in a class by themselves. Those who lived in the late 1800's and the early 1900's are rapidly disappearing and with them goes a part of Arnprior's history. And so this document hopes to preserve their memory and their memories for those who follow. Here are a few of these beloved *"characters"*.

ERNEST B. WOLFF

If you don't know him but if you see a rather short, distinguished looking (youthfully-elderly) gentleman, sporting a cane, walking briskly along John Street, stature erect, that's Ernie Wolff, a man who possesses all and more of the inherent qualities that make up a *"character"* of our time. With only limited formal education Wolff must be classed among the most highly self-educated people in our midst. His knowledge of history is not limited to local events; he is capable of discussing intelligently all of the nation's Prime Ministers since Confederation. An authority on British history, he can talk about their leaders and their politics back hundreds of years. An avid reader, his tremendous knowledge comes from his study of up to one thousand volumes of the best books available, a veritable library in his possession. A musician of note, Ernie Wolff was one of the finest trumpet players in the musical world of his day. He was a member of practically all Arnprior bands down through the years and an excellent singer. Ernie worked at McLachlin's No. 3 mill from age 12 to 18. He loved listening and talking with old-timers and he recalls Alex Yuill, a jackladder operator, who had actually seen Archibald McNab the Last Laird of the Clan McNab.

Ernie Wolff has performed yeoman service to his community in many ways and in particular his 30 years of faithful service as a member of the Arnprior Cemetery Board of Trustees. He usually had charge of organizing the Memorial Services on Decoration Day, an annual event held the last Sunday in August. A regular Hansard subscriber, Wolff is an authority on parliamentary procedure and a master at chairing a meeting. The possessor of a keen mind and remarkable memory, Ernie has to be classed as one of the best historians, not alone in Arnprior, but a recognized authority on the district as well. Wolff can relate a story in an entertaining and amusing manner. He is a man of strong conviction and is capable of intellectual discussion on practically every subject. Ernie and his wife Olive live at their Landrigan Street home where Mrs. Wolff has one of the more beautiful flower and vegetable gardens in the community. A son, Carl, is a Professor at Brock University in the Department of History.

President Ernie and Olive Wolff
Occasion Historical Society Dinner

R. A. JEFFERY

Former owner and publisher of the Arnprior Chronicle and one-time Mayor of Arnprior, Jeffery was a counterpart of Ernest B. Wolff in that he too was a self-educated man. According to his nephew, J. W. C. Tierney, Jeffery had not, or just did pass his High School entrance examinations, but nevertheless went on to become one of the finest orators ever developed in the Valley and one of the most successful newspaper men of his time. When demanded, he could take an editorial stand and rake the local Town Council over the grid. Back in 1914 Jeffery wrote editorially of the dust problem on Arnprior's main street. Describing it as *"fearful"* he said, *"The populace will rise up and call that councillor blessed who will move to have the sprinkling wagon out on John Street on Sunday morning and again Sunday evening for at least one trip up and down the street."* He added, *"It is unnecessary that everybody who cares to go to church should have to eat the proverbial peck of dirt each Sunday."*

Although a man of strong principle and conviction, he was also a diplomat. He wrote a scorching editorial back in April 1912 along the following lines: About 1909 the WCTU sponsored a drinking fountain on Elgin Street near the junction with John Street and in the words of Jeffery, *"With commendable zeal for the general good of the public and with a spirit of philanthropy, presented to the Town of Arnprior, a drinking fountain for man and beast."* But that is where Jefffery ceased to be diplomatic and forgot the niceties. In a strong editorial plea to town council he deplored the fact that the fountain, *"with its common cup of brass for all"* was a terrible health hazard not only to adults but to the hundreds of school children who used *"the ugly brass cup"*. Continuing Jeffrey said, *"let the animals drink there, if you will, but if adults and children must satisfy their thirst at the fountain it would be better for them to get down and drink out of the horse trough — away with the filthy, disease breeding common cup."* The power of the press won out, the old *"man and horse"* fountain was removed.

Elgin St. 1910. Note drinking fountain.

EDGAR HARRINGTON BURWASH

A young looking 91, Burwash is another of Arnprior's unique "characters". Burwash perhaps might well have both feet in heaven. Edgar is an Anglican, but his great, great, great Grandmother is a Roman Catholic Saint, Elizabeth Ann Bayley Seton, a 19th century convert to Catholicism following the death of her husband and founder of the Sisters of Charity. Elizabeth Ann Bayley Seton was beatified by Pope John XXIII on St. Patrick's Day, March 17, 1963 and on September 14, 1975 Pope Paul VI issued a decree of canonization on her behalf and she became America's first native born Saint. And there are two Anglican bishops, great, great, great uncles of Edgar, buried in a Cathedral in England and another Roman Catholic bishop who was a son of Saint Elizabeth Ann Seton.

Edgar was born in the McLachlin built frame mansion on John Street where the Sullivan homes now are; then lived for years in another McLachlin constructed home, the large brick residence on John Street presently Sacred Heart Convent. Edgar's father, John H. Burwash, Vice-President of McLachlin Brothers, purchased the large brick residence of Eric Harrington on William Street, now owned by Gerald and Douglas Macklem, where the family lived

Edgar Burwash in his garden, 1983

Burwash children, Edgar in foreground covering holes in knees of stockings, 1897. Photo front of Burwash home, now Sacred Heart Convent.

for sometime before moving to the big frame residence once located adjacent to the McLachlin office. Burwash served as an officer in both World Wars. He likes to reminisce on bygone days when as a youngster he played out the battle of the *"Modder"* (South African) vintage, in the field where presently stands St. Joseph's school. Edgar's mother was the former Ethel Mary Seton Hardinge of Portage du Fort. Nostalgically, Edgar likes to tell that it was at the little white gate leading into the *"Edgewood"* estate that his father proposed marriage to his mother.

For some time Burwash worked with McLachlin Brothers. He tells many stories one of which was when he was doing some work on the tug-boat *"Jean Macnamara"* moored at the *"boom"* camp. The bearings had gone on the bow roller and Burwash was endeavouring to cut off the worn parts using a hammer and chisel. He looked up and noticed a horse and buggy coming along the road. It was George Johnson, the chief engineer. Johnson came down to the boat and said *"You'll never get it cut that way — give me that hammer."* Johnson swung, the boat lurched and the hammer hit his hand. He threw the chisel up into the bush and the hammer into the lake and left. Edgar Burwash can relate many interesting yarns of the past and loves to reminsce on that long gone era. He is married to the former Eleanor Reid Farmer. They reside in a Burwash home on Ottawa Street.

C. A. MULVIHILL, K.C. AND
CONLIN S. MULVIHILL, Q.C.

A flamboyant type, Cornelius Anthony Mulvihill left his mark on Arnprior. He was Mayor of Arnprior during the terms 1928-29 and again in 1932-34. His election as Chief Magistrate in 1932 was the result of the most hectic mayoralty battle ever in Arnprior. Mulvihill and Stafford R. Rudd seemed constant political rivals for the top post in the community. In 1928 Mulvihill polled 645 votes while Rudd had 468. Again in 1929 Mulvihill won but his majority was reduced; he received 672 votes while Rudd polled 541. Mulvihill retired at the end of 1929 and Rudd secured acclamations for 1930 and 1931. But in January 1932 both were back at it again. The election ended in a tie, each polling 711 votes. Rudd, the incumbent, claimed he had priority by virtue of alleged precedence. However, the question went to the town solicitor, Trevor H. Grout, who talked with both contestants. The result — the Town Clerk-Treasurer G. H. Moles cast the deciding vote in favour of Mulvihill.

When he died at a relatively early age, Mulvihill had been very active in all community projects. He not only left an indelible impression on the populace of Arnprior but he also left his son, Conlin Sheridan Mulvihill who also became a lawyer and took over his father's business. The younger Con possessed all the attributes of his father together with a great regard for the *"little man — the little guy"* who always got a big smile and hello on a first name basis from the tall, distinguished looking lawyer. Had not death intervened, Conlin Sheridan Mulvihill had a most promising career ahead of him. His passing was indeed a sad blow to his town and its people.

JAMES MUNRO SR.

Jim Munro has been well described as a *"homespun philosopher"*. One of Arnprior's old-timers said, *"There was no one else in town like Jim Munro"*. A native of Arnprior, Munro operated a butcher shop in his building on the corner of Daniel Street and Rock Lane. After retirement he was a familiar figure sitting out front, always ready to converse with old friends and passers-by. He liked people and frequently crossed Daniel Street to visit with his friend, blacksmith Tom Cotie with whom he spun tales. Referring to Munro, someone said, *"He was very down to earth, one about whom Mark Twain would probably have written a novel."* Munro recalled the era when Elgin Street was principally a long row of vegetable gardens. A keen sportsman, he sponsored a hockey team known as *"Munro's Pets"*. He was very fond of horses and kept two in stables back of his shop. He possessed a sort of *"cracker barrel"* philosophy and had a penchant for needling people good-naturedly. The story is told that Munro liked to drop in to the J. K. Whitelaw Grocery store on Elgin Street. Mrs. Whitelaw, said to be a very assertive woman who chewed gum incessantly, became involved in a discussion with Munro that prompted her to quip, *"Munro, if I had a husband like you I'd poison him"* and Munro is said to have shot back, *"And if I had a wife like you I'd take it."*

Munro was among the first shareholders in the Galetta Electric Power Corporation along with John Brennan and Tom Moran. Truly, Jim Munro was one of the fine characters of his day in Arnprior.

N. ALAN CAMPBELL

N. Alan Campbell, former President of Neil Campbell Limited, is without doubt one of Arnprior's great story tellers. He loves to talk and he knows how to relate his experiences in a most entertaining manner. Known to everyone as *"Sculler"*, only a few people are aware as to how he picked up that moniker. Campbell cannot recall who labelled him with it but here's the story: During the summer of 1925 Alan and some other fellows went over to Norway Bay to a dance via the steamboat *"Norvic"*. The ferry boat operated until midnight. The dance over, Campbell escorted his girl friend home and then began hiking back to the dock only to lose his way in the dark among the numerous side roads and cottages that still exist at the Bay. He finally made it only to find the *"Norvic"* tied up for the night. The steamboat Captain told Alan where he might commandeer a row boat and the *"Norvic"*

N. Allan Campbell, 1983

would tow it back next morning. He got the boat and oars O.K. but in so doing awakened the owner. Campbell was in front about 100 yards and rowing like an Eton crew member on the Thames River, with the owner in hot pursuit in a canoe and armed with a .22 rifle. Alan evaded the pursuit and rowed the three miles across Chats Lake to Sand Point and then walked six miles down the railway track to Arnprior. That's how he got the nickname, "Sculler".

Campbell has been connected with all phases of sport in some capacity. While attending Queen's University he actually went a couple of rounds with "Frenchie" Belanger the Canadian Featherweight Boxing Champion. Belanger was in Kingston attending a seminar and agreed to a boxing exhibition at the University. They offered twenty dollars to anyone who would spar with Belanger for three rounds. Alan was a member of the University boxing team and he wanted that twenty bucks so he volunteered. "Frenchie" and "Sculler" worked out a gentleman's agreement that would at least make the sparring match look good. But in the first round "Sculler" became overly ambitious. They sparred a bit and threw a few light hooks, then the "Sculler" thought he saw an opening and the wild thought flashed through his brain — "imagine if I could knock out 'Frenchie' Belanger". Campbell's brain did him in. In the next round he again thought he saw the opening and laced Belanger with a real dandy. That was it, the "Sculler" awakened as they were carrying him to the dressing room. Alan and his wife, Doris, reside in their spacious Poole Street home replete with a beautiful swimming pool, where the "Sculler" reclines and reminisces about the good old days.

JOSEPH POULIOT

Joseph Pouliot, a sprightly 95-year-old, who likes to ramble on about the good old days when he loaded frames in No. 3 sawmill which he describes as "one hell of a job". Weighing just 150 pounds at the time, Joe said, "I tailed the Big Stock" perhaps the toughest job in the system. He recalls being paid $1.95 per day loading frames, "a tough job for a youngster". The lumber proceeded along a conveyor to be graded, then the frame-loader man-handled the heavy green red pine "deals", sometimes up to eighteen feet in length and six inches thick. Pouliot began working at McLachlin's at age 14 piling pickets and worked the lumbering company's shanties at age 16 including the old-time "camboose". He worked as "cookee" for chef Ben Seguin, a job that necessitated getting out of the "sack" at five o'clock every morning. Recalling McLachlin chief engineer George Johnson, Pouliot said, "Johnson knew his business but money was no object — look at that big engine in No. 3 — that damn thing must have cost a million bucks — the main drive belt was many feet in length and six to eight feet wide, solid leather."

"Saturday night eventually became the big night in town", said Joe. "McLachlins originally paid on Thursday but too many men got drunk and would not show up for work next day so the company switched pay day to Saturday." He recalls when there were seven hotels in Arnprior and two liquor stores. "There were lots of fights in the hotels when the drinking became heavy." Joe, who enjoys a drop of the "Poteen" himself, said, "One could buy a glass of liquor for five cents and six glasses of beer for twenty-five cents." He recalls Napoleon Lavoie working on McLachlin steamboats and as a millwright in No. 3 sawmill. "He was a powerful man," said Joe, "that's what killed him, lifting something that was too heavy." It was said Lavoie carried an unusually heavy object up a long stairway from the millwright's position beneath the mill, an object that ordinarily required two men to lift. Pouliot gets a kick out of recalling some amusing incidents in his life. Prior to waterwork installations in the town, Joe remembers pumping water from a well through a wooden trough, probably made of hewed out half logs, to the cistern in the Roman Catholic rectory at the time of Father Chaine's pastorate and commenting on this said, "What a hell of a job that was — I put in a hell of a lot of time on that damn pump."

Pouliot finally left McLachlins and went to Kenwood Mills in 1922 remaining there until his retirement. He said, "It was the best move I ever made, only place I made a dollar, steady work year round, 33 years of it." He loves to play cards — "I like a good game of euchre — I like to gamble too but I'm very unlucky, I'd lose my shirt." Joe is in good health other than a hearing impairment. He uses a cane which his son Michael brought from the Korean war theatre and says "If it wasn't for this damn sore back I'd be alright — one hell of a time getting up in the morning — I can't walk at all."

Joseph Pouliot, 1983, former McLachlin employee

Lavoie collection

ART GRENIER AND JIMMY GRAHAM

Both excellent camp chefs, *"beans in the sand"* vintage. Charles Macnamara once lamented that the time had passed when cooks knew how to bake beans in the sand. Art and Jimmy were good at it and Jimmy is still around to show anyone how it should be done. Both these fellows are in the *"character"* class. Jimmy likes to tell the story of the time when he and Art had a bit of a disagreement as to the proper method of preparing beans for baking in the sand. It was at the Grenier cottage at the foot of Chats Lake. They made the fire pit, had it really glowing ready for the pots to be placed and covered but the argument occurred as to the proper method of preparing the beans. Here is the story as related by Graham and confirmed by Art's son, Donald.

Neither was satisfied with one pot of beans — they had to have their individual pots. As Jimmy was preparing his, Art interrupted with the comment, *"What are you doing?"* Graham replied, *"Getting the beans ready for baking."* Art countered, *"That's not the way to make beans — I make them like Uncle Alphonse used to in the shanty — boil the beans until the skin breaks, then throw out the water and pour fresh water on the beans add salt pork, a layer of beans a layer of pork, until the pot is filled, then place heavy brown paper over the top of the pot and place the lid on."* Graham replied, *"Uncle Alphonse didn't teach me — my mother taught me and this is the way it's done. Boil the beans, then drain the water or stock into the bean pot with the beans, add a tablespoon of molasses, salt and pepper, tablespoon of brown sugar and a 'pinch' of mustard."* Both pots were placed in the pit and covered.

The following day both containers were placed on the table and everyone helped himself *"camboose"* style. Now here's the *"downer"*. Young Donald took some of his father's then sampled Jimmy's and out poured the *"plunker"* — *"You know Dad, Jimmy's beans are better than yours."* Donald kept on eating — Art's face dropped and Jimmy added insult to injury when he said, *"What do you think of that?"* Jimmy thought the whole thing was cruel, but inadvertent. In subsequent bean baking Grenier changed his style and used the Graham recipe.

Oldtimers Jimmy Graham and Art Grenier preparing pit for beans in the sand.

MRS. LEAH HACHEY

A fighter for the rights of little people, as was Leah Hachey, an outstanding example of a fluently bilingual Canadian and while she enjoyed visiting the home of her birth, Bagotville, Quebec, she was first and foremost a Canadian at heart. The former Leah Gagnon was born June 6, 1884 and moved with her parents to Arnprior in 1890 during the exodus of Quebec lumbermen to Arnprior to join the lumbering operations of the then internationally known McLachlin Brothers. Educated in Arnprior, she married Victor Hachey, also one of the hundreds who came from Quebec and New Brunswick to work with McLachlins.

Leah Hachey became a sort of legend in Arnprior as a battler for the little people. Many of the former Mayors knew and liked her; she did not bother with subordinates but had a knack of responsive communication with the top brass. Mrs. Hachey witnessed the rise and decline of the lumbering era. Most of her life was lived on Harriet and Albert Streets. An avid reader, she also loved sports and went to bed early but only after having a tiny drop of her favorite 5-Star brandy. The couple had nine children. The only surviving member is Georgette Hachey Mantil who resides in the homestead.

Mrs. Leah Hachey, one of Arnprior's Grand Old Ladies.

ALEX STAYE

Perhaps the best way in which to describe Alex Staye is *"a modern Horatio Alger"* who became, by his ingenuity, a recognized Ottawa Valley entrepreneur. An astute businessman, a great community minded citizen and perhaps above all, a respected advisor and companion to many elderly gentlemen in the area, Alex did not always have it so good. As a 13-year-old, Staye slung heavy white pine lumber in McLachlin's No. 3 sawmill. Big and strong at that tender age, Alex recalls *"tailing"* the gates, one of the toughest jobs in the operation. He remembers the writer's father whom he claims was *"tall, dark, always with a ready smile"* quite young at the time and employed as a millwright, kidding with the youngsters and remarking to Alex, who was perhaps tiring a bit on the job, *"Your backside is getting pretty close to the ground."*

Hiring youngsters was not quite according to the law, but because of the war, adults were scarce and the kids wanted to work. Alex recalls hiding in the nearby bush when it was known a labor inspector was making a routine check. It was a 10 hour day, six days a week, 13 hours each day including the walk to and from work.

Staye built and operated the *"Mayfair"* dance pavilion for 31 years. Among the famous bands playing the *"Mayfair"* were Syd Fox and his Hotel Diana from Kingston with Edith Dunne soloist and the renowned Berkley Kidd orchestra with soloist Norma Locke. This band worked the Chateau Laurier, Banff Springs Hotel and Lake Louise. In latter years Del Hudson with Tom McElligott Jr. at the piano were regulars. Alex Staye is very active and always ready to support worthwhile projects in his home town and district.

Alex Staye

Photo by Hanson

Reproduction by Hanson

Farmer Bros. store early 1900's. Left to right: Edwin Farmer, William "Cy" McCann, Arthur Farmer and Evan Farmer. Boy in forefront Marcel "Bidou" Clouthier.

Farmer Bros. Boot-making staff, 1924.

EVAN FARMER

The patriarch of the oldest active shoe store in Canada is indeed among the fine characters in Arnprior history. The Farmer business, now 115 years in operation, is in its third generation of management by the family oriented firm. Farmer enjoys reminiscing on the bygone days in Arnprior and likes to recall when Arnprior's plank constructed sidewalks were pitted by the caulk marks of the log-drivers' boots — boots that often were made in the Farmer boot-making shop located at the rear of the store. The business was founded in 1868 by William Farmer, Evan's uncle. Farmer brought his brother John, an expert boot maker, into the business and added Walter Duhn, Edward Nieman, Tom Robinson and Duncan Dagenais to the boot-making staff. Another brother, Edwin, Evan's father, entered the business and in 1916 purchased full control of the firm. The second generation of the Farmer family became involved when Arthur, son of Edwin, joined his father about 1917 and the second son, Evan, entered the business in 1922. Arthur died in 1958 and shortly thereafter the present partners in the business, Douglas and Donald, joined their father Evan and assumed full control when he retired a few years ago. A keen sportsman, Evan Farmer starred on local baseball and hockey teams and was a member of the famed Arnprior Alerts school-boy hockey squad. An ardent fisherman, Evan Farmer likes to tell of the days long ago when he fished area creeks for speckled trout usually with success. A second baseman with the Cabinet Factory team, Evan chuckles as he tells the story of the All Star Arnprior team playing in a Labour Day tournament at Kingdon Mine with teams from the Mine and Renfrew. It seems one of the Arnprior players was without a uniform. The former American professional, now the coach of the All Star squad, "Gus" Long, solved the problem quickly. Long disappeared into the dressing tent and shortly emerged in his "long Johns" and handed his uniform to the player.

Very respected and prominent citizens of the community, Evan and his wife Margaret reside in their John Street home.

TALES BY CHARLIE "MAC"

CHARLIE MACNAMARA kept a little black book in his pocket at all times. In this book are recorded some of his experiences while tramping the trail to his cabin at Marshall's Bay . These short accounts contained much information about his journeys around the district. In one, he tells of a Sunday, August 1, 1926 trip to High Falls with friend Liguori Gormley. Back roads were quite primitive in those days, plenty of big stones protruding and on one of these the car broke down. Awaiting a tow truck from Calabogie, Macnamara tells of his conversation with an elderly Algonquin Indian. In the course of the conversation Macnamara told the Indian that he worked with McLachlin Brothers and the Indian repeated slowly and thoughtfully: *"Dan, Hugh, Jack, Claude"*. He had also worked for McLachlins. The Indian also said he had known John T. Wait and the Postmaster Andrew Russell.

Some of the stories Macnamara recalls are: *"J. A. McManus giving foreman Brisson Epsom salts instead of strychnine to poison wolves"*, and *"Joe Seguin, a very good cook but he was in a camp one winter where he (Seguin) had a spite against a man and he nearly poisoned the whole gang with bad cooking trying to get even with the lad he did not like."* Another story tells of a big fight in a hotel between a gang of *"raftsmen"* led by a burly log-driver, who were stationed at the point at the mouth of the Madawaska River and a group of Pakenham battlers headed by Allan Carswell and James McAdam. The fight raged all over the lower floor and out in front of the building. The story goes that the *"raftsmen"* were finally driven out and retreated to their camp on the point.

And another story tells of the March 7, 1937 swim by Krikor Hakamen. Here is how Macnamara describes it: *"A young travelling Assyrian, commercializing his resistance to cold, went in swimming in the open water below the cement bridge (of old time — the 'Mill' Bridge) on Sunday afternoon, March 7, before a gathering of 1500 spectators. The collection he took up before his dip is said to have come to $40."*

And Macnamara tells of a rash and foolhardy act by four young men who, on June 6, 1925, ran a river boat over one of the gates in the *"Mill"* Bridge. The boat capsized but the men were saved. They were trying to duplicate a feat the day previous when a boat piloted by an old Indian had run the same chute without difficulty.

CHARLES HORNIDGE

An Irishman with lots of intestinal fortitude, for at the age of 19 he and his wife Cecelia Finn, emigrated from Ireland to make a new life in Canada. But when the young couple arrived in the forest wilderness they were so disappointed and lonesome that they wanted to return to Ireland but could not raise the money for the homeward journey and so had to remain. Charles and Mrs. Hornidge were a fine couple and Arnprior benefited much from the Hornidge family's forced decision to remain.

It was during the height of the McLachlin lumbering era that Hornidge arrived in Arnprior. He was hired as Coachman and later assumed the position of chief gardener. Eventually he became gardener for S. D. Hall owner of *"Edgewood"* estate. A son, Richard age 93, lives at Aylmer, Quebec. A granddaughter, Dorothy McCabe, recalls much of her younger years living with her grandparents in the large chief gardener's house at *"Edgewood"*. Charlie threw many a scare into the young fellows who climbed the high board fences to steal apples and grapes at *"Edgewood"* but he never really did much about it other than to chase them

and if he succeeded in catching anyone they received a reprimand and were released. Alan Campbell was one of those Hornidge caught up in an apple tree. Alan recalls Hornidge giving him a tongue lashing and putting him in a hot greenhouse for a session of sweating, then letting him go with the admonition *"Don't let me catch you here again."*

Edgewood chief gardener Charlie Hornidge with pal Tony and front wheel drive bicycle.

PHILIP DONTIGNY

Philip Dontigny was one-time partner in the firm of Dontigny & Hughton and later sole owner of the woolen mill located on the site where now stands the senior citizen apartment building between Burwash and Madawaska Streets. The original plant, of frame construction, was destroyed by fire in 1885 and a new brick factory was built. They manufactured fine grey flannels which were marketed throughout Canada. The mill had a manufacturing capacity of one thousand yards per day.

Dontigny, who was something of a *"curmudgeon"*, was one of the great characters of his day. An avid movie goer, he attended almost all the movies, silent in his day. But Dontigny, an effervescent type, was not too silent; during exciting Western movies it is said he would shout and pound his cane on the theatre floor. A daughter, Olive Dontigny Gormley, was one of the most outstanding singers in Canada. A soprano, it was said that she possessed Metropolitan Opera qualifications but instead chose marriage and home life in Arnprior.

JAMES AND EVANGELINE MOSKOS

Those who were kids in the early 1920's remember nostalgically Jim and Evangeline Moskos and their Sugar Bowl Candy Kitchen. The Moskos loved kids and many were the youngsters who received free ice cream cones or candy from the highly respected couple; kind little gestures that kids never forget.

There's a real human interest story involving Jim and Evangeline. They were friends in Greece, but Jim, in 1889, as a very young boy, left his homeland alone for America to make his way in the new world. Paying his own steamship passage, he landed in New York and made his way to Baltimore where he remained for three years. Following a stint in Montreal he went on to Toronto where he learned the confectionery business with an elderly Greek gentleman. In 1914 Jim and his brother Chris opened a confectionery store in Prescott and in the same year Jim came to Arnprior and formed the business then known as the Sugar Bowl Candy Kitchen, located in a building between Ben's TV and the One Hour Cleaners.

In 1922 Jim travelled to Montreal to meet his former girl friend and bride to be, Evangeline Matthews. They were married in the Greek Orthodox Church in Montreal.

In 1923 the Campbell House burned and in 1925 Moskos bought that corner property and M. Sullivan & Son built what is now known as the Moskos Block. Jim Moskos was a philosopher in his own right. He loved people, and his wife Evangeline, with her always ready smile, was an excellent partner. The couple had three children, Peter and Leo, who still operate the business under the name Sugar Bowl Restaurant, and Constantina, Mrs. Tina Bedford, who resides in Belleville. Jim Moskos died in 1966 and Mrs. Moskos passed away in 1978 but their kindly characteristics live on in Peter and Leo both well respected citizens of Arnprior.

ARNPRIOR POST OFFICE AND POSTMASTERS

THE HISTORY of postal service in Arnprior dates back to July 6, 1841 when, according to Canada Post Corporate Communications records, the first Postmaster was one Isaac Gregory, who apparently served in this capacity until 1853. However, an old newspaper article mentions the first Post Office serving the people of this community was situated on the site of the Jamieson farm in Fitzroy with the Postmaster being David Goodwin.

The second Postmaster in Arnprior was Andrew Russell, who along with his wife Jean McCowan, left Scotland in 1832 and came to Arnprior where they were welcomed by Chief McNab. The couple later moved to Pakenham and in 1853 returned to Arnprior where Russell was appointed Postmaster that same year. He remained in that position until September 30, 1869. This second Post Office was located in a building on the northwest corner of Daniel and Elgin Streets at which point Russell and his family also operated a general store.

Arnprior's third Postmaster was A. H. Dowswell who assumed the office on January 1, 1870 but resigned the position on March 31 that same year. This third Post Office was located on the northwest corner of Harriet and Elgin Streets, now the Federal Building property.

Esra A. Bates was appointed Arnprior's fourth Post-master on May 1, 1870 remaining in that position until August 11, 1891. It is thought Bates operated the Post Office from a building located on Hugh Street and owned by R. G. Moles.

The next Post Office location was at the southeast corner of Madawaska and Harriet Streets now the Becker store site. The office was later moved to the Galvin Block, the brick building on Elgin Street presently Berry's Farm Store.

The fifth Postmaster was Edouard deRenzy, appointed November 30, 1891, remaining in that position until his death in 1911.

It was in 1896 that the new stone Post Office structure now the D. A. Gillies building, housing the Library and Museum, was built. Following the death of deRenzy, one of his daughters carried on as an interim acting Postmaster until the appointment of H. W. W. Gardner on September 2, 1913. Gardner, the community's sixth Postmaster, continued until retirement on June 6, 1939.

Arnprior's seventh Postmaster was Hubert C. Gardner, son of H. W. W. Gardner. He was appointed February 1, 1940 and remained in office until January 22, 1944.

Mary Graham was appointed the town's eighth Postmaster in an acting capacity on March 25, 1944.

It was on January 15, 1947 that Ian G. Malloch became Arnprior's ninth Postmaster remaining so until retirement. Malloch and his staff moved into the new Federal Building on April 29, 1963.

Malloch was succeeded by the town's tenth Postmaster, Vern M. Morris, in January 1975. Morris remained in the position until January 31, 1978.

The eleventh Postmaster, Morley A. Galt, was appointed to the office February 1, 1978.

The present Postmaster, the twelfth, Bob Gallipeau, was appointed March 1982.

ANCIENT MUNICIPAL BYLAWS

A SEARCH OF town records discloses some interesting bylaws approved by Councils since 1862 when it was incorporated as a village and after it received town status in 1892.

Back on May 17, 1883, the Council of the day passed a bylaw appointing the first Street Inspector for the community. It reads: *"Bylaw No. 185 — To appoint John Martin to the office Street Inspector for the municipality of Arnprior for the period of six months from the first day of May. Therefore, the Municipal Council of the village of Arnprior enacts as follows: That John Martin be and he is hereby appointed to the office of Street Inspector of this Corporation for the term of six months from the first day of May 1883. That for the due performance of his said duty as Street Inspector he shall be paid the sum of thirty-five dollars. That the duties of said Inspector shall consist of supervising the construction of sidewalks and repairs on streets and sidewalks: to see that the same are kept clear of all kinds of obstructions and in a clean and proper condition."*

Another Bylaw No. 149 passed April 25, 1878 has 17 clauses. Here are a few:

"1. *That it shall not be lawful for any person or persons to play at marbles, cricket, skittels, ball, racket, or any other noisy game, or to gamble with dice or otherwise, or to run races on foot or on horse back, or in carriages or vehicles of any kind, or to drive at a furious rate in any of the streets in any manner whatsoever or to dance or to play profane music on Sunday within the said village.*

"2. *That it shall not be lawful for any person or persons to go out fishing, hunting or shooting, or in quest of, or to take, kill or destroy any deer or game or any other wild animal or wild fowl or bird or fish or use any dog or use or carry any gun or knife or other engine, or any fishing rod, net or trap for the above mentioned purpose, except in defence of his or her life or property from any wolf or other ravenous beast or bird on Sunday within this village.*

"3. *That it shall not be lawful to sell or give intoxicating drinks of any sort or kind to any apprentice, servant, idiot, insane person or child within the village, without the consent of the master, legal protector, physician or parent of such person or child.*

"4. *That it shall not be lawful for any person to circulate or post any indecent placards, writing or picture, or write any indecent words or make any indecent pictures or drawings on any walls, fences, or any other place whatsoever, or to circulate the same within this village.*

"5. *That it shall not be lawful for any person to use any profane swearing, obscene, blasphemous or grossly insulting language, nor be guilty of any other immorality in streets, highways or public places, nor of any indecency therein, nor in private residences within this village.*

"6. *That it shall not be lawful to bathe, or indecently expose his or her person by washing in any water within this village, lying or running near any public highway or dwelling house between the hours of six o'clock in the morning and nine o'clock in the evening, unless provided with and clothed in a proper bathing dress sufficient to prevent any indecent exposure of his or her person.*"

The penalty for violations was, "*either to be committed to the village lockup for a time not exceeding ten days, or to the 'Common Gaol of the County of Renfrew' there to be imprisoned for any term not exceeding thirty days or to be liable to a fine of not more than twenty dollars.*"

Bylaw No. 74 approved on September 14, 1896, was to authorize the imposition of wharfage dues and rents for use of the wharf and storehouse situated at the north end of John Street. In part, this bylaw "*deemed advisable and proper to charge the owners or masters of steamboats a reasonable sum per annum for the privilege of using said wharf and storehouse by tying or otherwise fastening such steamboats to the said wharf and for the storing of goods or merchandise within the said storehouse; that a charge of eighteen dollars for the summer season be paid*" for this privilege.

Bylaw No. 8 dated April 5, 1893 appointed Henry Dodd Chief Constable, with other part-time constables on

call. Apparently these part-time constables were paid fifteen cents per hour for services performed between 7 a.m. and 10 p.m. and twenty cents per hour between 10 p.m. and 7 a.m.

Bylaw No. 12 June 16, 1893 gave permission to the Automatic Telephone & Electric Company of Canada to erect telephone poles and wires for furnishing telephone service, this for a term of twenty years.

Bylaw No. 13 May 7, 1895, termed a "*scavaging bylaw*", stated: "*No privy or water closet shall be used in this Corporation unless the same shall have, for the reception of deposits, a substantial box made of good lumber with a door in the end or side thereof, easily opened and easily accessible to the public scavenger; the contents of all privies and water closets must be removed from the premises at least every three months between the first of April and the first of December each year.*"

Another 1893 bylaw stated in part: "*That no person shall expectorate tobacco juice or throw any objectionable matter or thing upon any person passing along or having business upon said streets.*"

Bylaw No. 98 December 15, 1897 appointed R. B. McCreary Engineer for the town as required by the "*Ditches and Watercourses Act*". McCreary's salary to be thirty cents per hour.

Bylaw No. 133 December 1, 1899 authorized a contract with the Arnprior Electric Light & Power Company to install 87 incandescent lamps on Arnprior streets in places designated by Council. The Arnprior Electric Light & Power Company powerhouse was a brick structure at the eastern end of Burwash Street.

Bylaw No. 144 April 5, 1893 states: "*No person shall shout or make any other unusual noise or any noise calculated to disturb the inhabitants of the Town of Arnprior on any street, nor shall any person take part in any CHARIVARI or other like disturbance of the peace in the Town of Arnprior.*" A dictionary definition of "*Charivari*" is a "*Shivaree*" and a "*Shivaree*" according to Webster is "*a noisy mock serenade to a newly married couple*"

Bylaw No. 148 July 6, 1900 was approved for the issue of debentures in the amount of $50,000 for the purpose of constructing and equipping waterworks within the town. Amortization from September 1, 1901 on through to September 1, 1930. Also under the same date Bylaw 149 was approved for the construction of sewers at a cost of $25,000, amortization same as above.

Bylaws Nos. 150 and 151 dated July 27, 1900 appointed Roberty Surtees, Civil Engineer, Ottawa, for the construction of waterworks and sewers. And for the purchase of land for site for Waterworks Pumping station from Michael Havey (pumphouse and water tower).

In the year 1910, Council was beseiged with requests for granolithic sidewalks throughout the town as well as sewer extensions and lighting. Council was still authorizing construction of board sidewalks in 1911 in certain areas.

Bylaw No. 418 October 1910 to authorize the grant of the right to the Galetta Electric Power & Milling Company Limited to supply electric power to Arnprior and to provide for the issue of Debentures for $6,000 for the purpose of making improvements and changes in connection with the waterworks system necessary owing to the proposed use of electric power in operating the said waterworks. Ratepayers voted on this with the result 211 For and 209 Against; carried by simple majority.

PROGRESS

BY THE year 1892 when the community officially received Town status, it was literally bursting at the seams with, of course, the lumber industry providing the impetus. Gravel covered streets replaced mud bogs and deep pot holes; sidewalks of plank were being constructed on most streets and granolithic walks were not far off. Churches and schools had been built; frame homes replaced log shanties; and brick constructed dwellings were also being erected particularly along John Street. Banks and many other business establishments were being set up (as early as 1863 there were some 41 business and professional people in Arnprior) and the town was classed among the most progressive in Canada.

During those early years, understandably, living conditions were primitive. Most houses were of log or frame construction; drinking water was drawn from a community well; oil lamps were in style; wood burning stoves were the primary method of heating and cooking. People *"banked"* their homes with sawdust prior to winter setting in. Outhouses were everywhere; people kept farm animals and fowl which promoted one old-timer to quip *"chicken every Sunday"*. The more fortunate constructed their own wells, installed cisterns in their homes which held rain water piped from roofs to the cistern and then to the kitchen by pump. Those among the affluent might have a septic tank and toilet facilities.

It was 1904 when the waterworks system was being installed in Arnprior. The Town Engineer at the time was Robert Riddell, a man of whom old-timers attest to his tremendous ability. One of these, George Parsons, a retired engineer and Queen's University graduate, recalls clearly the honeycomb of deep excavations on the streets in 1904 and 1905 at the time of the water and sewer construction program. The pumphouse with its two steam pumps was located just below the present water filtration plant. Original operators were John Forbes and Tom Payne. No one manned the pumphouse at night; the day operator would pump the tanks full for the night. The operator lived nearby and if the fire alarm sounded during the night he would hurry to the pumphouse to ensure ample water supply was available.

Work on the water and sewer project was done by hand, pick and shovel. Parsons recalls Charles W. Powell, one-time prominent citizen and plumber, who came from Kingston to Arnprior. Powell told of his delight in working on the clean, new, modern equipment in Arnprior in contrast to the Kingston water system where some wooden pipe installations were still in use.

There were accidents during that period of construction. One such tragic event resulting in the death of one man and the miraculous recovery of another occurred during the installation of water and sewer services on Daniel Street.

Harvey Fulton, whose father Andrew Fulton, was on the scene almost immediately after the dynamite blast, describes it as related to him by his dad. Andrew Fulton, who boarded at the O'Neill House then situated on the corner of Elgin and Daniel Streets, was seated out front talking with another gentleman when a terrific blast, emanating from a deep trench on Daniel Street, shook the area. Fulton knew there were two men in the trench; one of them, John Watson, was lying there with an iron bar protruding from his back; the other man had portions of a hand blown off by the blast. The man with the badly mutilated hand was taken by freight train to Ottawa where he died in hospital. Watson pleaded to be taken to his home on Charles Street. His wish was granted, but there was little hope for his recovery. According to grandson Harold Watson, the iron bar pierced his grandfather's body just below the rib cage, missing the heart area by one inch and emerged through the back below the shoulder blade. The story goes that Dr. James G. Cranston fastened a tube presumably for draining the wound; then drew the the bar from the body. Watson lived to tell his grandsons Harold and Howard of the episode. He died at age 89. It is thought that the men were using the metal bar to tamp down powder when it promoted a spark setting off the charge.

THE CHIEF MAGISTRATES

ARNPRIOR HAS been most fortunate in having many outstanding people occupy the office of Chief Magistrate down through the years. As mentioned earlier, the community was incorporated as a village in July 1862 with Eric Harrington as Reeve. It did not claim town status until 1892 although it had ample population by 1882 to receive a town charter.

The following is a complete list of Arnprior Mayors from 1892 to the present day as well as some population statistics at various stages of time.

1892	John Harvey
1893	R. G. Moles or John Harvey
1894-1896	R. G. Moles
1897-1898	B. V. Stafford
1899	M. D. Graham
1900	W. M. Howe
1901	Claude McLachlin
1902	Samuel Kedey
1903	John Harvey
1904-1905	J. G. Cranston Dr.
1906-1907	W. M. Howe
1908-1912	Dan McLachlin
1913-1914	John Brennan
1915-1918	W. A. Cameron Dr.
1919	T. S. Church

1920	W. A. Cameron Dr.		1958	5,435
1921-1923	W. H. Steele Dr.		1959	5,510
1924-1925	R. A. Jeffery		1960	5,530
1926-1927	E. D. Osborne		1961	5,533
1928-1929	C. A. Mulivihill		1962	5,546
1930-1931	S. R. Rudd		1963	5,662
1932-1934	C. A. Mulvihill		1964	5,566
1935-1936	W. H. Moore		1965	5,532
1937	J. R. McQuigge		1966	5,534
1938-1945	A. H. Reid Dr.		1967	5,650
1946-1947	A. A. McLean		1968	5,733
1948	S. R. Rudd		1969	5,766
1949-1962	R. M. Simpson		1970	5,807
1963	G. S. Levy		1971	5,966
1964-1965	R. M. Simpson		1972	6,017
1966	W. E. Prentice		1973	6,230
1967	G. S. Levy		1974	6,109
1968-1969	G. T. Fitzpatrick		1975	6,109
1970-1974	H. T. Cranston		1976	6,059
1975-1980	G. M. Johnson		1977	5,915
1981-1984	T. E. Sullivan		1978	5,911
			1979	5,806
			1980	5,806

It is interesting to note that R. M. *"Bob"* Simpson served as Mayor of Arnprior for a total of 16 years. Simpson deserves much credit along with his Council of the day for the persuasive industrial expansion program that resulted in the establishment of several new and large industries in Arnprior.

A native of Arnprior, Dr. A. H. Reid served with great distinction as Chief Magistrate for 8 very trying years in that period 1938-1945.

Another native born citizen of Arnprior, Hugh T. Cranston, was Mayor of Arnprior for 5 years, in addition to 27 years as a member of Council serving in various capacities, for a total of 32 years.

George M. Johnson, a very intelligent personage, noted for his firmness and vigorous stands, resisting stress under pressure in policy matters which he thought were beneficial to the town as a whole, served as Mayor of Arnprior for 6 years; this in addition to another five years as a member of Council.

ARNPRIOR POPULATION FIGURES 1897-1980

Year	Population
1897	3,746
1901	3,937
1902	3,791
1905	3,907
1926	4,197
1950	4,336
1951	4,499
1952	4,530
1953	4,600
1954	4,829
1955	4,930
1956	5,375
1957	5,375

The year 1973 Arnprior posted the largest population in its history up to and including 1980, with a count of 6,230 people.

REEVES OF ARNPRIOR

FOLLOWING ARNPRIOR'S incorporation as a village in 1862 and up to the period when the community received Town status in 1892, the Reeve was the top position on the municipal Council. The following is a list of those people who have served in the office of Reeve of Arnprior to the present time:

1863-1864	Eric Harrington
1865	A. H. Dowswell
1866-1867	John Harvey
1868-1871	Eric Harrington
1872-1873	William Carss
1874	Eric Harrington
1875	John Tierney
1876-1878	Eric Harrington
1879	John Harvey
1880-1885	Richard Dulmage
1886-1892	R. G. Moles
1893	David Craig
1894	Arthur Burwash
1895	John Harvey
1896	Simon Kedey
1897-1898	W. J. Johnston
1899	M. D. Graham
1900	W. M. Howe
1901	Claude McLachlin
1902	Simon Kedey
1903	G. Delahaye

1904-1905	Dr. J. G. Cranston
1906	W. M. Howe
1907-1908	W. J. Johnston
1909	W. M. Howe
1910-1911	Edwin Farmer
1912	John Brennan
1913-1914	Dr. W. A. Cameron
1915	Alex Reid
1916-1917-1918	John Brennan
1919	James McPherson
1920	Dr. W. H. Steele
1921-1922	S. S. Tripp
1923	R. A. Jeffery
1924	James Gaudette
1925	A. D. F. Campbell
1926	J. R. McQuigge
1927	James B. Jack
1928	J. R. McQuigge
1929-1936	T. S. Church
1937	Dr. A. H. Reid
1938-1944	John Moran
1945	A. Steel Campbell
1946	S. R. Rudd
1947-1948	R. M. Simpson
1949-1950	Maurice T. Sullivan
1951-1961	Charles W. Wagenblass
1962-1965	J. Biggs Jack
1966-1972	Thomas E. Sullivan
1973-1974	Henry Murdoch
1975	Wilfred Frieday
1976-1980	J. E. Sadler
1981-1984	William R. Price

The following are the Reeves of Arnprior who served in the office of Warden of Renfrew County: Eric Harrington; R. G. Moles; W. J. Johnston; John Brennan; T. S. Church.

SCHOOLS

PUBLIC SCHOOLS

Perhaps the most knowledgeable person with reference to the early Public School system in Arnprior is Mrs. Myra Lindsay. At 89 years of age, Myra loves to relate stories of her many years teaching in local schools. Possessing a terrific sense of humor, she spices the conversation with anecdotes that bring laughter to the listener. A resident of *"The Grove"*, Myra quite often has former pupils come to visit her. Recently a fellow walked into her room saying, *"Hello Mrs. Lindsay."* Myra replied, *"I know that smile — does 'razor blade' mean anything to you?"* Her visitor quickly replied, *"It sure does."* Apparently many long years ago the then youngster swallowed half a safety razor blade while doing some soap sculpturing. Although not in Lindsay's room, Myra was called to the scene; a doctor arrived and the boy was taken to the Ottawa Civic Hospital and what could have been a serious situation was averted. This is just one of scores of interesting tales that Myra

Lindsay can quickly call to mind. She has taught well over one thousand pupils during her career. She recalls Principals John *"Barney"* Gillespie and, of course, Walter A. Zadow who was Principal for 25 years and in whose honor the school is named. Walter Zadow was among the most popular of the school Principals in Arnprior. His wife, Mae, also served as Secretary-Treasurer for 12 years.

According to Myra, the early Public Schools were located on the east side of Daniel Street between Elgin and the bridge. The first was in an area across from the present Oddfellow's Hall and when the enrollment increased, the upper storey of the present machine shop on the corner of Daniel and Rock Lane was utilized as a school. It was in the period about 1860 that a large two-storey brick school was built on Ottawa Street. This was the building which housed the *"Great Railway Celebration"* in December 1864 when the Brockville & Ottawa Railway reached Arnprior. On February 1, 1925 the Public School was levelled by fire and for a year the student body was scattered throughout the town utilizing every available space.

The upper floor of St. John Chrysostom school, consisting of four classrooms, was turned over to them. The vacant upper rooms over business places were used and in some cases heating problems presented themselves. Within a year a new eight classroom brick school was built, the cornerstone of which was placed on June 10, 1925 by Henry Cockshutt, Lieutenant Governor of Ontario. In 1952 a new wing was added at which time Walter Zadow was Principal and Alex Reid Secretary-Treasurer. In 1972 a third wing was added and officially opened on May 23, 1973 by the Deputy Minister of Education, Dr. E. E. Stewart. At that time Principals were T. W. Harkins and D. J. Fraser.

Alexander Reid School, named in honor of long time Secretary-Treasurer and Chairman of the Board of Education, Alex Reid, was built in 1957 and opened for students in September of that year. It was officially opened February 18, 1958 by the Honorable Matthew Diamond, Minister of Health. Eva Brown was the first Principal, with Walter Zadow Supervising Principal. Another two room addition was built in September 1967. The final addition, consisting of two classrooms, one kindergarten room and a gymnasium, was built and opened to students in September 1969, with the official opening in January 1970. The second Principal at Alexander Reid School was Donald Lyon, a native of Arnprior, who served in that capacity from September 1963 to June 1983. He then joined the staff of McNab Public School. Lyon was succeeded by Gary Pettigrew.

SEPARATE SCHOOLS

It was in 1876 during the pastorate of Rev. J. A. M. Chaine that the four classroom two-storey brick St. John Chrysostom School on Albert Street was constructed and some years later another equivalent section was added to bring the total to eight classrooms.

The school was staffed by lay teachers prior to the arrival of the Sisters of Charity of Halifax in 1896. This Order remained until 1907 and it was in 1909 that the present Order, the Sisters of Providence of St. Vincent de Paul, arrived in Arnprior principally as teaching Sisters. The schools are now staffed by lay teachers with only two Sisters remaining on the faculty. There were very few conveniences in those early days. Jack Murphy, with dry Irish wit, remarks: *"No inside toilets — the girls had the better facilities — a small brick building; the boys an old wooden shack on the side of the hill — I well remember it, particularly in winter."* The large frame McLachlin built home fronting John Street, between Church and Lake Streets, was acquired for use as a Convent. After the purchase of the present brick Convent, also a McLachlin built structure, across John Street, the frame building was then used as a four classroom school supplementing St. John Chrysostom's. This was known as St. Bernard's and was during the pastorate of Monsignor Bernard J. Kiernan. The present St. Joseph's School was opened to the students on January 8, 1951. Monsignor J. T. Warnock was Parish Priest at the time. The official opening was that summer 1951 when the school was blessed by the Most Rev. W. J. Smith, Bishop of Pembroke and formally opened by Premier Leslie Frost. Also attending were Ontario Hydro Commission Chairman, Robert Saunders; Minister of National Revenue, Dr. J. J. McCann; and Mayor R. M. Simpson. It was in 1964, during Monsignor R. E. Dillon's tenure, that John XXIII School was built to serve children of the fast growing southern area of town. This was officially opened by the Honorable William Stewart. It was also blessed by Bishop Smith. Both St. Joseph's and John XXIII have undergone extensive expansion programs since original construction. Sister Nancy Wilson is Principal at St. Joseph's and Robert Daze Principal at John XXIII.

ARNPRIOR DISTRICT HIGH SCHOOL

Remember that old song, *"Kiss Me Once, Kiss Me Twice and Kiss Me Once Again, It's Been a Long, Long Time?"*

The last six words in that famous song hit could well have been the theme of the Arnprior District High School during the 1976 year-long celebration of the 100th Anniversary of its founding. Hundreds of people travelled 100 years down memory lane that Saturday night in February 1976 to help the Arnprior District High School celebrate its 100th Anniversary at the first of two huge banquets, part of the year-long festivities.

The late Conlin S. Mulvihill, Q.C. introduced Judge Edward Houston at the head table presentations. Both are natives of Arnprior and attended local schools. And Anne Graham, affectionately known as *"Dot"*, faculty member for many years, now retired and living in Arnprior, brought the house down with a laughter filled history of the early days of Arnprior High. Known as one of the finest staff members ever to teach in Arnprior, one who while always fair, maintained strong discipline, Graham prompted a tremendous roar from the crowd when guest speaker, Doctor Stewart *"Sandy"* MacGregor, related the story of the inebriated local chap staggering up to Graham as she sat in her

parked car on John Street and slurred out the words, *"Miss Graham, I want to thank you for all you did for me at school, you made me what I am today."* *"Dot"* Graham and her sister Jean, also a well respected former member of the school teaching staff, are perhaps the best historians on matters relative to the Arnprior School. As a very young girl, *"Dot"* came home to teach in 1919, the year the school adopted the present motto, *"Hodie non Cras"* — *"Today not Tomorrow"*.

One-time student and member of a family synonymous with Arnprior, Monte Cranston, drew a laugh when he gingerly referred to Miss Graham saying, *"I think I can now call you 'Dot'"*. But the roof blew off when Judge Houston approached the mike shortly thereafter and quipped, *"I'm certainly not going to call her 'Dot' because I'm still afraid of her."*

It was a night of good natured banter. There was a social hour replete with bar, licensed of course, prior to dinner and Principal Bill Sly overheard some of his former pupils remark — *"This is really not fun — we had more fun years ago drinking beer in the washrooms."* And many recall sneaking into the furnace room to steal a smoke if one could dodge the caretaker. One of the great mathematics teachers of that era was Ella Gillan Rogers, an outstanding mathematician with sound discipline. School faculty member and band-leader, Ted Graham, went back many years to play period music of those memorable years. Bonnie Bews, Ken Dodge and E. A. *"Murph"* McIntyre organized and chaired the programs.

Much of the information relative to this article on the Arnprior District High School is derived from the book entitled, *"A Short History of the Arnprior High School"* by A. H. D. Ross, 1865-1922, a former Principal of the school. Among others, Ross acknowledges the valuable contributions to his history by *"Malcolm D. Graham, the efficient and courteous Secretary-Treasurer of the Arnprior Board of Education."* Graham who is the father of Anne and Jean Graham, was Secretary-Treasurer for 25 years. Ross traces the history from the establishment of the Arnprior Grammar School in 1865 under Headmaster James Muir who received his appointment in August of that year at a salary of $500 per annum.

Among the first pupils were: Wilson Bangs, Zebba Bangs, Blanche Blaisdell, Harriett Blaisdell, Armon Burwash, Edgar Burwash, John Burwash, Archie Campbell, Lucy Carss, James Craig, Martha Dean, Augusta Hackett, Emma Hackett, Nellie Hackett, Isabella Jane Halliday, James Halliday, Mary Jane Heath, Dugald Keddie, Kate Leishman, John Lindsay, Mauray Mackie, Hugh McDiarmid, Kate McDiarmid, Isabella McFarlane, William McKay, Jessie McLachlin, Mary McLachlin, Kate McPhee, William O'Connor and Mary Kate Rowe.

In his book, Ross states: *"From August to December 1865 Mr. Muir and his students occupied a room on the west side of a partition running across the lower flat of what is now known as the Old Public School building at the* northeast corner of Ottawa and Hamilton Streets — the entrance being from Harriet Street." From January to July 1966 the Grammar School occupied the upper flat.

The second Headmaster was Henry L. Slack who abolished the use of slates. Students made their own exercise books from paper obtained at the *"Arnprior News"*. Slack received $600 per year. They subsequently occupied rooms on Harriet Street north of Victoria; later moving to a frame building on the west side of Harrington Street and then to the northwest corner of Madawaska and Harriet Streets.

In 1871 William C. Middleton became Headmaster and the name of the Arnprior Grammar School was changed to the Arnprior High School. They then occupied a section of an addition to the Old Public School. The first lady teacher, Miss Emily R. Patterson, was appointed in January 1873, at a salary of $250 per year.

In 1873 the High School students were again crowded out of the Public School and took up quarters in a frame building facing Albert Street which was owned by the Methodist Church (probably the present Walter Boswell residence). During the first ten years the school operated from ten different locations. Ross states: *"To put an end to this wandering around in the wilderness, the Board of Education decided to take vigorous action."* On February 2, 1875 a committee consisting of Dr. J. G. Cranston, Chairman of the Board; George Craig, Secretary; and John Tierney, Treasurer, were requested to select a suitable site for a High School. The property chosen was that upon which the present High School stands. On June 23, 1875 a contract for the erection of the new four-room brick building designed by Architect Hodgson, was let to Stafford, McCreary & McMartin, at the price of $6,212.

Subsequent Principals were: Findlay Ferguson Macnab in 1878; Richard Dawson, 1883; Lewis C. Corbett, 1884-1891; Barclay Craig, 1891-1895. Among Craig's pupils were, Percival J. Cooney, author of *"Kinsmen"*, Charles Macnamara, noted Ottawa Valley naturalist and historian; Jennie A. Cranston, Walter Tierney and George Valin. The 8th Principal was J. W. Grey 1895-1897, followed by William de Geer Johnson, Archibald E. Morrow and in January 1905 to June 1910, George E. Mabee, followed by W. E. Rand who remained until June 1919.

It was in 1910 that a large addition was built to the north of the building erected thirty-five years previously. The new wing cost $14,338.

In September 1919 Alexander Herbert Douglas Ross took over as Principal until 1922, followed by T. M.

Henry for a short time, after which George William Rudlen assumed control, followed by A. R. Scott who was appointed Principal in 1926 serving until 1935 when A. C. Ward, a native of Arnprior, became Principal, remaining until 1964 when Principal William H. Sly took over. The present Principal is Borden Wallace.

The school became the Arnprior District High School in January 1948. The last vestige of the old school, the section that at one time was the original building, was destroyed in the fire of July 1977. Extensive renovations and additional construction followed.

In addition to a tremendous athletic program, the school boasts one of the finest drama clubs in the province. Under the direction of staff members, Stuart Morrison and Arlene Avdovich, both of whom are talented actors and directors, the school has won several Valley and Provincial honors.

Among the outstanding graduates of the Arnprior High School are, Percival J. Cooney, author of *"Kinsmen"*, who became a teaching Professor and Director of Americanization at the El Monte, California University. He was one of the twenty thousand select who were listed in *"Who's Who in America"* at the time. Cooney visited Arnprior in 1929. He died March 17, 1932 at the age of 61. A brother, Frank, who once worked in the E. C. Armand Grocery and who eventually became a large grocer wholesaler in Montana, was elected Governor of that State in November 1932 as the Democratic candidate, winning by a majority of 17,000 votes. John W. Dafoe, former editor of the Winnipeg Free Press attended High School in Arnprior. His fellow students christened him *"Shakespeare"* because of his scholarly achievements even at the age of 12 years. Dafoe was once described by Senator Grattan O'Leary one-time publisher of the Ottawa Journal, as, *"with the beginning of an editorial career which for influence and prestige and independence has had no parallel in Canada in our time"*. Another graduate who achieved nation-wide success was D. C. Coleman, former President of the Canadian Pacific Railway. Of course there were many others too numerous to mention, who have brought honor and distinction to their alma mater.

It's been a long, long time and much has transpired since that January in 1876 when Principal William C. Middleton led his student body of 49 girls and 31 boys into the original building around which many subsequent additions have arisen to make it one of the most modern educational centres in the country.

Walter Zadow Public School

Alexander Reid Public School

St. Joseph's Separate School

John XXIII Separate School

Arnprior District High School

Photo by Hanson ©

THE INDUSTRIAL REVOLUTION

FOR ALL intents and purposes, Industrial Arnprior was McLachlin Brothers from 1851 until 1929. This statement is made with all deference to Huyck Canada Limited which firm came into being in Arnprior in July 1918 under the name of Kenwood Mills Limited, the Canadian subsidiary plant of F. C. Huyck & Son with headquarters in Albany, New York. Everyone living in Arnprior during the years of the Great Depression remember what Kenwood Mills meant to the community from that 1929 period which saw the shutdown of McLachlin Brothers who for so long was the town's major industry.

There were also a few smaller plants in the community at the time but when one considers a company employing up to 1000 men in a town that in 1929 had a population of 4,500, then the closing of such an industry must have had a devastating effect on the entire community. Under these circumstances Kenwood Mills literally saved Arnprior from becoming a ghost town. And so, commencing in 1918, although no one thought of it as such, the Industrial Revolution began in Arnprior, a period of industrial diversification continuing to the present day, that has made Arnprior one of the more classic examples of a community realizing the importance of varied operations in the industrial field.

HUYCK CANADA LIMITED

PRIOR TO acquisition in 1918 by the Huyck people, the brick factory involved in the transaction, known as the Griffith & McNaughton plant, had some historical significance. It was about 1915 that Jim Griffith of Lachute, Quebec and Norman Lewis McNaughton (father of Arnprior's Catherine McNaughton) commenced operation in a frame building on Elgin Street manufacturing socks for the Canadian army. Shortly thereafter they purchased the former Shirt Factory, a brick structure built about 1908 which burned about 1910. The building was located on Bassett Street, between Edward and McDonald Streets, a roadway leading to the Edward Bassett residence. Griffith & McNaughton repaired the building and again began the manufacture of socks and blankets for the army. At this point in time there was no drying apparatus in the plant and they devised a unique method of drying blanket cloth. The material was partially dried with a spinner system and then finished outside. An arrangement made of wooden posts, seven feet high braced by two by fours, top and bottom, in about ten foot sections, held lengths of blanket material about 75 feet long which were hooked both top and bottom on the frames and left to dry. Weather conditions dictated when the cloth was hung out for drying.

It was in July of 1918 that Huyck purchased the Griffith & McNaughton mill. The plant was incorporated as Kenwood Mills Limited, perpetuating the name of the earlier Huyck location in New York State. This expansion into Canada was a natural because of the booming paper industry in Canada. Arnprior was also a natural location due to its proximity to the Canadian paper industry as well as the quality of water which was necessary for wool scouring and good felt fulling.

The advantageous tariff regulations affecting Canada resulted in the concentration of substantially all of Huyck's export felt business in Arnprior. It remains so today, even though the company have other plants covering some of the countries to which they export.

The Company grew and changes were inevitable. Additions to the plant became necessary and new equipment was added. When suitable synthetic fibres and chemical treatments became available they were used scientifically to improve the performance of the felts. As these changes were introduced the name of Huyck became more widely known in the market place, so in 1962 the firm's name was changed to Huyck Canada Limited, with two divisions; Kenwood Mills in Arnprior and Formex Company of Canada in Kentville. In 1967 these divisions were combined and operated under the name of Huyck Canada Limited with headquarters in Arnprior.

In 1980, B.T.R., a world-wide conglomerate with headquarters in England, purchased Huyck Corporation including all its divisions. The name of Huyck Canada Limited has been retained. Expansion and changes have continued and as a result, Huyck Canada Limited has maintained a position of leadership in the market for Wet Press Felts and Forming Fabrics. This significant achievement results from the combined efforts of all employees to manufacture products of technical superiority which are ready when the customer needs them.

Up until a few years ago the company manufactured the world renowned Kenwood wool blanket and wool cloth with which some of the nation's most prominent tailoring firms made Kenwood overcoats, a garment which, while light, was extremely warm and well suited for Canadian winters.

Edmund N. Huyck was the first official President of what is now Huyck Canada. The first Executive Manager was Holden M. Ashby, while the first Arnprior resident to manage the company was Woolsey W. Weed. Other Presidents in order of service are: Harold A. Short, Wyatt Dick, Kirke H. Dunlap, Jack K. Melville, E. J. Sielewicz, R. F. Faircloth, M. Mayes, G. D. Verge, A. J. E. Lawson and again G. D. Verge.

Some years ago the film "The Town and The Mill", a technicolor production by Crawley Films, Ottawa and narrated by Andy Clarke, was produced. The film depicts the complete process and manufacture of the raw material to the finished felt and wool blankets that Huyck then manufactured, as well as various shots of local scenes throughout the town.

M. SULLIVAN & SON LIMITED

ONE OF THE few companies with an exclusive Arnprior background, M. Sullivan & Son Limited can be traced back in history to the square timber era. The company was founded in 1914 by Maurice Sullivan who had personally achieved an outstanding reputation as a builder. The family tradition of sound workmanship was already established by Maurice's father, who had erected many domestic and farm buildings using timbers that he had squared himself.

Photo courtesy M. T. Sullivan

St. Thomas Anglican Church, Woodlawn. Contractor Maurice Sullivan, firm's founder, standing highest point, steeple.

Maurice Sullivan, the first President, committed the company to maintain this family tradition by a demanding philosophy based on the idea that any building erected by his firm should last as long as the materials with which it was built could survive. As younger members of the family enter the firm, they are thoroughly indoctrinated with the family traditions thus maintaining the company's integrity and dependability over the years.

Their first contract was the construction of the St. Thomas Anglican Church, Woodlawn, built by the founder Maurice Sullivan.

The firm is one of the few Canadian contracting companies that has remained entirely in the hands of the founding family for so many years. All key positions in the company are occupied by highly trained members of the family or by trusted employees with a long background in the firm. The Sullivan philosophy of the frequent introduction of younger men into the organization also keeps the company oriented to modern, progressive attitudes.

The strong family tradition on which the business philosophy of M. Sullivan & Son is based, demands strict adherence to the highest concepts of quality, design, finish and time schedules. The success of these enduring qualities is aptly expressed in the record of the company and the recommendation of its clients down through the years and their policy has helped make them one of the largest and better known companies in Canada. Specialists in the construction of schools, colleges, churches, universities, hospitals and other such institutions, M. Sullivan & Son Limited has completed a remarkable variety of contracts throughout Canada. In addition to the above, they have built hotels, motels, theatres, factories, office buildings, bridges, water treatment plants, pollution control plants, mass housing projects, as well as facilities for Hydro, Bell Telephone, Canadian Pacific, Canadian National and the Armed Forces. Client satisfaction has been well proven by the fact that the Sullivan firm is usually called on to make renovations or additions to original structures which they have built as changes become necessary over the years.

Very community minded and proud of their home town of Arnprior, the Sullivan firm has constructed many local institutions and are always willing to offer advice when requested. The Sullivan Industrial park, where many of Arnprior's newer industries are located, was made possible by the three senior members of the firm, Harry, Dominic and Mort Sullivan.

The present executive members of the Sullivan firm are: Honorary Chairman, J. D. Sullivan; Chairman, M. T. Sullivan; Vice-Chairman, G. M. Johnson; President, H. P. MacMaster; Secretary-Treasurer, J. D. Sullivan Jr.; Executive Vice-President, Engineering, D. G. McDonald; Vice-President, Atlantic Operations, W. D. Reid; Vice-President, Finance, W. D. Holmes; Vice-Presidents, A. E. Sullivan, T. E. Sullivan, Ian MacMaster; Comptroller, L. C. Armstrong.

Arnprior Builders Supplies, with John Kuash as General Manager, is also an integral part of the Sullivan enterprise.

SMITHS CONSTRUCTION COMPANY

ANOTHER COMPANY with roots in their home community of Arnprior, the Smith Construction Company, recognized as one of the bigger highway construction firms in Ontario, is perhaps one of the more family-oriented companies in Canada. The Chief Executive Officers of the firm are the three brothers, William Smith, President; Frank Smith, Vice-President; and Nicholas Smith, Secretary-Treasurer. Also occupying prominent positions in the company are Bill's four sons, Dan, John, Allan and Tom; Frank's two boys, Frank Jr. and David; and Nick's son, Peter.

Smiths Construction giant Caterpillar Scooper Shovel. Left to right: Nicholas Smith, Secretary-Treasurer and William Smith, President.

The Smiths have come a long way since that day back in 1933 when in the midst of the Great Depression Bill and Frank decided to venture into business in a world deep in a state of economic collapse. The boys bought a truck and working out of the homestead on Elgin Street, took every type of trucking job that would bring dollars.

They hauled sand, gravel, top soil and every other commodity, gradually building a business from scratch. There must have been a certain quality of intuition and foresight in the brains of the Smith Brothers because they saw the days of the *"horse and buggy"* were gone and the age of *"a world on wheels"* was fast approaching. And with those *"wheels"* there had to be highways and to build those highways there had to be knowledgeable road construction people and the Smiths were determined to be among the best in the business. In those pre-war years the world was talking about the great German autobahn expressways and Smiths foresaw, no doubt, the day when such super highways would be constructed in Canada.

Their fleet of trucks began to grow; they began their paving operation in 1941 and were successful in their bid for their first Department of Highways contract just five years later. From that point on they never stopped. They constructed a new office on Madawaska Boulevard and moved their plant and equipment to adjacent grounds in 1949.

But World War II interfered with the Smith plans when the younger brother Nick, who was destined for an executive post in the company, joined the Royal Canadian Air Force and in 1940, after pilot training, went overseas as a bomber pilot. After 33 operational missions over enemy territory, he then served as an instructor in England from 1943 until he returned home on leave in August 1944 with rank of Squadron Leader. He went back to England as an instructor remaining there until his return to Canada in October 1945. Nick joined his brothers and became Secretary-Treasurer of the company.

So extensive is their operational equipment and plant facilities that it is estimated it would cost about $12 million to replace in today's market. One of their most recent acquisitions is a Caterpillar Scooper Shovel. The machine, costing $500,000, has a bucket about seven feet high that can handle four and one half cubic yards of material. The Smith operation has a permanent work force of sixty people and a peak force of 350 people.

The rise of the Smith Construction Company from that modest beginning back in 1933 to their present outstanding rating in the highway building field is almost phenomenal and along with that climb they have achieved an outstanding reputation for reliability and efficient workmanship.

NOR-SAND METAL INCORPORATED

AMONG THE more recent and largest industrial acquisitions in Arnprior is the Nor-Sand Metal Inc. plant situated in the Sullivan Industrial Park. It was in September 1977 that the new plant, then known as the Special Metals Division of Noranda Metal Industries, was officially opened by the then Postmaster General, Jean-Jacques Blais.

The 155,000 square foot plant was established to supply much of the special tubing requirements of the CANDU and other nuclear reactor systems. Members of the federal and provincial governments, as well as representatives of power utilities and the nuclear energy industry, were among guests who watched as Blais, assisted by Noranda Mines Executive Vice-President A. H. Zimmerman, pressed a button charging a billet of metal into the pre-heating furnace as the initial step in extruding specialized tubing. The first Vice-President and General Manager of the plant was Dr. George Wilenius.

The plant represents a capital investment of $30 million and has employed up to 240 engineers, production, maintenance and administrative people. It was the first integrated Canadian facility designed to supply the nuclear power generating industry with high quality tubular components, especially for steam generation and fuel containment. It produces zirconium alloy fuel cladding, nickel alloy and speciality steel steam generator, heat exchanger and condensor tubing. In addition, speciality tubing is produced for other diverse applications including the petrochemical industry. The facility, completed in 1975, was designed to produce annually a total of seven million feet of nickel alloy steam generator and zirconium fuel cladding. While much of the production from the early years was exported to the United States, the plant became the main supplier of steam generator tubing for the CANDU nuclear generator sys-

tems. Production facilities ran at full capacity through 1979. A fall-off in nuclear construction coincided with a major change in the structure of the plant in January 1981. A new company called Nor-Sand Metals Inc. was formed with joint ownership 50/50 by Noranda Metal Industries Ltd. and Sandvik Canada Corporation. This company owns the building, property, nickel production facilities, engineering, laboratory and office units. At the same time, the zirconium operation was sold to Canadian General Electric who manage the unit with a work force supplied by Nor-Sand. The President of Nor-Sand Metal Inc. is W. B. Ferguson and the Vice-President, Operations is U. A. Matinlassi. The manager of the CGE Arnprior operation is Walter Tarasuk.

The Noranda-Sandvik move brought together the technical background of Sandvik's parent company in Sweden along with the modern Noranda Production facility. As a result of this move, the Nor-Sand plant, in addition to producing steam generators for the Canadian nuclear plants, is the main supplier of stainless steel pipe and tube to Sandvik Canada Corporation. In addition a sizeable portion of the stainless product is sold in the export market.

BADISCHE CANADA LIMITED

CONSTRUCTION STARTED in May 1965 for Union Carbide's nylon filament production facility. The plant was completed during the summer of 1966 with a work force of nearly 130 employees.

Henry Pero served as first General Manager, followed by Doug Bishop and then Dick Hughes who held this position just prior to the facility's acquisition by then Dow Badische Company. Ron Morgan was the first Plant Manager, a position he held from October 4, 1965 to December 31, 1976. Morgan is now Plant Manager for Huyck Canada Limited. The next Plant Manager was Larry Marshall who holds this position today.

In its earlier years, Union Carbide's Arnprior Plant made fine denier nylon filament for apparel and uses as well as products for the carpet industry, for upholstery fabrics, tire cord and for other industrial uses such as applications in seat belts, fish nets, tents, etc. In keeping with changing market requirements, the Arnprior Plant has concentrated its primary efforts on the production of nylon carpet yarns.

Union Carbide's Arnprior Plant was purchased by then Dow Badische Company, a joint venture involving two large chemical companies: Dow Chemical and BASF of West Germany. Drawing on the human and technical resources of the former Union Carbide operation, Dow Badische Canada Limited began a new effort to make these locally produced carpet yarns among the best in Canada. New marketing strategies were undertaken and a sales and administrative staff moved into headquarters in Ottawa.

From late 1974 until 1978, Arnprior's nylon production plant upgraded its equipment, while the wholly owned subsidiary was still part of Dow Badische. In May 1978 Dow Badische was fully acquired by BASF and the Company in the United States became known as Badische Corporation, while its Canadian subsidiary became Badische Canada Limited. By concentrating on continued development and marketing of speciality products, particularly into Zeftron R nylon range for the commercial carpet market, Badische Canada Limited continues to be a major supplier to the Canadian carpet mills. Today the plant employs about 270 people. Yarns produced at Badische Canada Limited's Arnprior Plant are incorporated in many famous carpet installations across Canada including the CP Head Office in Vancouver; Texaco Building in Calgary; Bank of Canada in Ottawa; the Royal York Hotel, Toronto; the Metro in Montreal and high traffic transportation installations.

PFIZER CANADA INC. ARNPRIOR PLANT

CHARLES PFIZER and a cousin Charles Erhart went to the United States from Germany, probably in 1848 and in 1849 they founded the Pfizer Company in Brooklyn, New York. The company has grown from that beginning to a world-wide organization with a multi-national work force of 40,000. In 1983 sales were in excess of three and one half billion U.S. dollars and facilities exist in approximately fifty countries in the world.

The Canadian operation was founded as a sales office in Montreal in 1951. Packaging operations followed and in 1955 the current Arnprior plant site of approximately 80 acres was purchased from the Herrick family. Plant construction occurred from 1955 though 1956; initial production began on June 25, 1956 and the formal opening of the Arnprior facility took place on Thursday, October 25, 1956. Initial productions were all various dosage forms of the antibiotic drug Terramycin, generically known as Ocytetracycline, discovered and patented by Pfizer in 1949 and which received U.S. Federal Drug Administration approval for sale on March 22, 1950. Early production consisted of sterile ampoules, vials and ointment, syrups, capsules and tablets.

This original plant was 24,000 square feet on one floor with a small *"penthouse"* machine room and employed approximately fifty personnel under the direction of Plant Manager Thomas J. Kolar. In 1963 Frank A. Rosar replaced Kolar as Plant Manager and has continued in this position to date of writing. A 16,000 square foot addition was added in 1968 and a further 5,000 square feet in 1976. In 1977 a multi-million dollar renovation of the entire facility was successfully completed.

Over the years new equipment has been added as new production technology developed and currently the plant is *"State of the Art"* and highly automated.

Current dosage forms produced of ethical drugs in several major therapeutic fields:

"Vibramycin"	— Antibiotic therapy
"Diabinese"	— Diabetes mellitus therapy
"Sinequan"	— Anti-depressant therapy
"Minipress"	— Hypertension therapy
"Antivert"	— Vertigo therapy
"Atarax"	— Anti-anxiety therapy
"Feldene"	— Anti-inflammatory therapy

At the end of 1983 a fully integrated, highly automated plant staffed with sixty employees under the direction of Plant Manager Frank A. Rosar, continues to produce millions of units of high quality ethical drugs.

BOEING OF CANADA LIMITED

BOEING OF Canada Limited, a Canadian subsidiary of the giant Boeing Aircraft Corporation is one of the great post-war industries to locate in Arnprior.

The current business charter of this company derived from the purchase by the Boeing Aircraft Corporation in 1961 and was established as Boeing of Canada Limited. Previous to this date the company had operated from 1954 as Piasecki Helicopter Corporation.

The prime role of this Division is to provide repair and overhaul support to Boeing-Vertol Helicopters in use by the Canadian Defence Forces. Logistics and spares support is also provided.

Since 1969, Boeing of Canada Ltd., Arnprior, has developed a high Machine and Sheet Metal skill in order to procure diversified business and maintain a large enough labor base to offer an attractive competitive rate. During this period of time, this Division has received off-load Machine and Sheet Metal work from Seattle, Philadelphia and Winnipeg, which proved our skills and resources.

In 1972, this Division concluded a two year support effort on a research and development program on the CH47 Helicopter (Chinook). The *"State-of-the-Art"* concept was in the search of a tactical air guidance system (T.A.G.S.).

In 1974, Boeing undertook the manufacture of Lag Dampers for the CH113/CH113A/107/CH46 Aircraft under a licensed agreement with Delco. The first production run went to the Operators in June 1975 subsequent to qualification tests.

The company employs 235 people. The facilities in floor area have grown from 43,000 square feet in 1954-69 to 103,000 square feet with the acquisition of the new facility.

The Managers of Boeing of Canada Limited, Arnprior Division, since 1954 have been: Jack Charlston, Ed Ritti, Max Bowen, Henry Burress, Dave Ely, Don McNeill, Archie King, George Montgomery and Ken Laver.

SQUARE D CANADA LIMITED

SQUARE D CANADA, Electrical Equipment Inc., with its World Corporate Headquarters located in Palestine, Illinois, was founded in the early days of the electrical industry and has grown to become a major manufacturer of electrical equipment operating more than seventy five production and warehousing facilities throughout the world. Through the years Square D has maintained a reputation for product excellence. Continued to the present day, it is a tradition made possible only by the constant and energetic efforts of more than 21,000 employees to meet or exceed high standards of quality in their every day work. The Square D name is synonymous with a most diversified line of equipment which is used to distribute and control electricity in homes, offices, stores, schools, farms and factories. Necessary to the operation of lights, machines, appliances and computers, these products make possible the many conveniences of modern day living and increase the efficiency of work.

Development of non-domestic markets for Square D equipment dates back to 1914 when the company opened a factory in Walkerville, Ontario to assemble safety switches. The initial success of this operation led to the organization of Square D Canada Limited ten years later. With headquarters now located in Mississauga, Ontario, the Canadian subsidiary includes manufacturing plants in Stratford, Port Colborne, Arnprior, Edmundston; assembly facilities in Waterloo, Montreal and Edmonton; warehouses in five locations and sales offices in seventeen cities.

In December 1974 Square D Canada Limited located in Arnprior, in the building previously occupied by Travellaire Company. Following extensive alterations to the facility, the plant began production in April 1975. The official opening was presided over by Mitchell P. Kartalia, Chairman of the Board and Chief Executive Officer of Square D Company, as well as Charles R. Verrier, Past President and General Manager and Member of the Board of Square D Company Canada Limited.

From the initial stages of planning until his transfer to Mississauga in October 1980, Bob Kendrigan was responsible for the Arnprior plant in his capacity of Plant Manager. Robert Larsen is presently Plant Manager.

The Arnprior plant plays a key role in the overall Canadian operation since it is a feeder plant to supply standard components to assembly plants in Waterloo, Montreal and Edmonton as well as several standard merchandise items to our warehouses. In addition, Arnprior engineers and manufactures I-Line Feeder and Plug-in Busway and the control units associated with this product as well as Motor Starter Racks and several other devices which are shipped directly to its customers and/or distributors.

The Arnprior plant presently employs sixty five people most of whom come from the towns of Arnprior, Renfrew and surrounding districts. The plant employees are represented by Local Union 1563 of the International Brotherhood of Electrical Workers AFL-CIO. The company maintains a policy of promotion from within and with few exceptions the supervisory staff is made up of local people.

The electrical industry being highly competitive, it is essential that the Arnprior plant operate in an efficient and reliable manner in order to keep an adequate supply of material going out to the assembly plants across Canada. This in turn contributes to attainment of the Company objective of: Giving the customer what he wants, when, where and how he wants it, at a price he is willing to pay and do it for a profit.

GILLIES BROTHERS & CO. LTD.

A SUCCESS STORY in terms of pioneer life, is again the oft-repeated tale of a Scottish family who were not afraid of hard work. It is a saga of taming the land and carving out a living in the wilderness.

John Gillies, at the age of nine, came to Canada with his parents in 1821. In due course he built a small water-driven sawmill five miles north of the village of Lanark at a place then called Gillies Mills now known as Herron's Mills. This was in 1842.

In 1862 he purchased the Gilmour limits on the Mississippi River and a sawmill at Carleton Place for his sons. In 1873 Gillies bought the newly established sawmill of the Rev. Henry Usborne at Braeside; with the mill was also purchased 200 square miles of timber limits on the Coulonge River. On July 4, 1910 fire destroyed the west lumber yard at Braeside containing 29 million board feet of lumber. The sawmill was not damaged. They were not so lucky, however, in 1919 when the Braeside mill burned down. In the autumn of 1920 a new electrically driven brick and concrete mill was erected. At that time it was the first fireproof mill of its kind in Canada.

In 1953 the company had upwards of 1800 square miles of timber limits on the watersheds of the Coulonge, Black and Schyan Rivers in Quebec and the Petawawa, Madawaska, Matabitchouan and Sturgeon Rivers in Ontario, all under lease from the Ontario and Quebec governments.

Back in the 1870's the Ottawa River was teeming with rafts of square timber. These timbers might have started any place, but usually they were on their way to Quebec and the British Admiralty. The British favored a sort of square cut timber, with the edges levelled off, thus creating a hexagonal type of timber. Tug boats were numerous on the Ottawa drawing big log "booms" at speeds of one mile per hour so as to prevent the logs from jumping the "boom". Gillies Temagami mill eventually closed and logs were water driven 200 miles to the Braeside plant. The Gillies mill was sold to Consolidated-Bathurst in November 1963.

Presidents down through the years were: James Gillies 1842-1909; John Gillies 1909-1914; David Gillies 1914-1926; John S. Gillies 1926-1938; David A. Gillies 1938-1959 and Chairman of the Board 1959-1961; John A. Gillies Jr. 1961-1962; Arnold G. Muirhead 1962-1968; W. W. "Bud" Gillespie 1968 until retirement with Consolidated-Bathurst.

DOCHART BRICK & TILE WORKS

THE DOCHART Brick & Tile Works was established by William Baker in 1868 on Lot 7 Concession 13, McNab Township and registered as Dochart Brick & Tile Works. The company used clay from their pits on the banks of the Dochart Creek. The widely known plant was operated by the Baker family from its inception in 1858 until 1947 at which time it was purchased by John S. McKay, a widely known entrepreneur from Baie Comeau, Quebec.

In 1951, McKay formed the Dochart Brick & Tile Company, Limited and the plant was rebuilt so as to specialize in the manufacture of the agriculture clay drain tile and the installation of same. They served principally the trade of Quebec and Eastern Ontario through to 1980.

The company was again re-organized in 1980 as Dochart Clay Products, a prime producer of clay flower pots, under the management of Peter T. McKay. The company presently supplies the large retail outlets in Canada from coast to coast. All products leave the plant in package form and are distributed by highway transport.

PLAYTEX LIMITED

PLAYTEX LIMITED has been a Canadian subsidiary plant of the parent company in the United States. Locating in Arnprior in 1953 partly because of the town's proximity to the nation's primary market areas and the availability of skilled help, the plant encompasses some 91,000 square feet with large employment.

CHASE NUCLEAR CANADA LIMITED

AMONG THE new facilities in the industrial field in Arnprior, Chase Nuclear Canada Limited are fabricators of zirconium alloy pressure tubing for nuclear reactor fuel channels, most of which are used in CANDU reactors. Chase Nuclear located in Arnprior in 1974.

HYPERNETICS LIMITED

HYPERNETICS LIMITED located in Arnprior in December 1972. The founders and chief executive officers are: Edward J. Mulvey, P.Eng., President and General Manager; Eric C. Ridgen, P.Eng., Secretary-Treasurer and Chief Engineer. The company is a high technology industry producing digital indicators for use in aircraft instruments, motion controls, transducers, special valves, and provides precision machining services.

CALCUTRON CORPORATION

CALCULTRON CORPORATION located in Arnprior in 1969 for the manufacture of precision tool equipment. The presence of potential customers already established in the area along with low overhead were factors in the company locating in Arnprior.

ISOLATION SYSTEMS LIMITED

ANOTHER INDUSTRY, Isolation Systems Limited, one of the foremost manufacturers and suppliers of hospital equipment in the country, is located in the former Measurement Engineering factory. Employing 21 people, Isolation Systems established their Arnprior plant about 1979. The Plant Manager is Robert Davlin.

BARRDAY DIVISION OF WHEELABRATOR CORPORATION OF CANADA LTD.

A MANUFACTURER OF industrial air filters, Barrday Division of Wheelabrator Corporation of Canada Limited arrived in Arnprior in July 1979. They also employ 21 people The Administrative Manager of the Plant is Colleen Borutski.

DIDAK MANUFACTURING LIMITED

AT THE TIME of writing, Arnprior's newest industry, Didak Manufacturing Limited, is under construction. The company, located in the Sullivan Industrial Park, will manufacture technical components which are used in various computer processing programs.

INDUSTRIES OF THE PAST

ALTHOUGH IT is not possible to publish all the industries that flourished and helped in the development of Arnprior, some recognition should be made of the contribution of these people. Those not mentioned, nevertheless, played a role in making Arnprior one of the better communities in the nation and this history acknowledges the significant role they played in bringing about the end result, the beautiful town we live in.

DONTIGNY WOOLLEN MILL

BUILT IN 1852 by Philip Dontigny and Andrew Hughton, the water-powered textile plant was the first such in Arnprior, growing along with the McLachlin enterprise. The three-storey brick structure was one of the oldest business establishments in the Ottawa Valley, beginning its march to textile prominence in the late 1800's, manufacturing flannels, wool blankets and worsted cloth. It was in 1905 that Philip Dontigny purchased the firm. He died in 1925 and the Dontigny Mills carried on for a time but ceased operations in 1929. It was located in the area between Madawaska and Burwash Streets where the Senior Citizen apartment building is presently standing.

The factory operated intermittently for a while. In 1932 it again began operations on a small scale under the management of Miller and McElroy but in 1935 it once more became dormant remaining so until 1938 when it again reopened for one year under the direction of Fred Cleroux. The structure, with its obsolete machinery, was rapidly deteriorating when purchased in 1940 by W. N. Thomson and A. D. Claman who once again began the task of rebuilding. The firm was re-named the Arnprior Mill Stock Company. The original machinery and equipment was dismantled and sold and replaced with new and modern machinery. A new boiler house, storage buildings and spinning room were added. This prosperity was short lived and the project finally closed down for good. The buildings fell into a dilapidated state and were demolished in January 1962.

ARNPRIOR PLANING MILL

IT WAS IN 1900 that Daniel McKay came to Arnprior from Middleville and purchased the Sash and Door factory located at the corner of William and Daniel Streets, presently the site of the Government Liquor Store. The plant at the time was owned and operated by Vincent Barnett. Daniel's brother, George, eventually became involved in the business as well.

McKay added a sawmill at the rear of the plant. The planing mill was located on the main floor while the sash and door works occupied the second storey. The one steam engine in the plant had formerly been a part of the Malloch Sawmill on the Dochart. In 1923 a cement block building replaced the wooden two-storey structure. At one time both McLachlin Brothers and Gillies Brothers hauled rough lumber to the McKay plant for planing. Some twenty men were employed in the plant among whom were Emile Woermke, Herman Woermke, Edward Shea and David Hodgins. In 1947 the business was sold to a Renfrew firm and later to the Baker Ford Agency. The structure was later destroyed by fire.

A daughter, Mabel McKay Simpson, tells an interesting human interest story involving her and her brother Hartley then age 7. The mill was built over a creek and Mabel recalls Hartley falling into the fast moving creek and being carried through a culvert under William Street. Mabel, also quite young, had the presence of mind to grab him before he went under the railway tracks.

DAVID CRAIG & SON

THE *"Pea Soup King of the Ottawa Valley"*. That is the affectionate tag hundreds of people tacked on W. Barclay Craig, one-time widely-known Ottawa Valley businessman, sportsman and in the kindliest terms, one of the characters of his day. Three generations of Craigs were involved in the business of manufacturing flour, blended foods, processing food grains, malting barley and of course soup peas.

The Craig firm in its day, perhaps unwittingly, did much to relate French Canadians with pea soup. At one time the Craigs were shipping enough choice boiling peas into Quebec to make eighteen million bowls of pea soup per year.

It was 1889 when David Craig began manufacturing flour in the old stone, McLachlin built, building on the western extremity of the bridge, a structure destroyed by fire, and Ontario Hydro demolishing the walls at the time of construction of the new bridge and weir. The Craig plant which was finally located between the Canadian Pacific and Canadian National Railway stations, was sold to D. R. Berry & Sons after more than 84 years in business.

CANADIAN PUBLIC BOOTH

A COMPANY, THEN known as the Arnprior Cabinet Company, was established about 1916 with R. J. Simpson as Manager and Harry Meagher, Superintendent. Originally the company manu-

factured furniture but later built all of the telephone booths used across Canada. In later years the plant became known as Canadian Public Booth and was under the management of Robert M. Simpson, long-time Mayor and Councillor in Arnprior. Prior to finally closing, the firm constructed various types of office furniture etc.

A. F. CAMPBELL & SON

THE DANIEL Street site for this plant was purchased by A. F. Campbell from Michael Havey in the earlier years of Arnprior. Operated as a sash and door factory, the business was later taken over by a son, A. D. F. Campbell, who operated it for many years. The company, under new ownership, is presently located on Highway 17 west of Arnprior.

OTHER INDUSTRIES OF THE PAST

AMONG OTHER old-time industries were the Arnprior Marble Factory, located in the vicinity of Russell and Meehan Streets; the Carss Shingle Mill at the southerly extremity of Carss Street; the Merrick Boat factory at the easterly end of Burwash Street; Ayling & Ramage boat builders on the site of the Madawaska Marina; the Thomas Toy Axe Factory; the Arnprior Box Company who in 1914 manufactured the *"Stronglite"* cheese box; the Butter Tub Factory; McLean & Malloch Feed Mill on Madawaska Street; the Clothes Pin Factory on the corner of William and Division Streets; and the Shirt Factory. There was also the Malloch Sawmill at the Dochart owned and operated by George Malloch, grandfather of Ian Malloch. A Sash and Door Factory was also operated by Malloch & Adams in the area of the Malloch Road cemetery and a railway siding was constructed from the sawmill to the CPR main line. The Malloch sawmill employed about one hundred men.

The above are some of the smaller industries that come to mind at time of writing. If any are omitted it is inadvertent.

ARNPRIOR & DISTRICT MEMORIAL HOSPITAL AND THE GROVE

ARNPRIOR AND District are indeed fortunate in having one of the finest health care units in the country but it did not come to pass without innumerable hours of research, dedication and enduring initiative by an energetic group of citizens led by Doctor J. Howard Box.

For many years prior to 1943, the Medical Profession and many civic minded citizens discussed the feasibility of establishing a hospital in Arnprior. Through the efforts of Dr. A. H. Reid, Mayor of Arnprior during the years 1938-1945, Daniel McLachlin was approached to ascertain if he would consider selling the McLachlin residence on John Street for the ultimate purpose of establishing a hospital on the site. The result of this contact was that on February 19, 1943, the house and parcel of land 250 feet by 300 feet was conveyed to the Town of Arnprior.

On May 10, 1943, a delegation consisting of Dr. Box, W. Barclay Craig and C. A. Mulvihill, addressed Town Council on behalf of the citizens of Arnprior and the following resolution was passed: *"That the Council apply to the Department of Health requesting them to send an inspector re. the feasibility of turning the McLachlin property into a hospital and, if so, the Mayor be authorized to obtain an architect, the cost of such an architect to be borne by the Corporation."*

The proposed project was subsequently checked out by the Department of Health and permission was granted to proceed. On October 7, 1943, Dr. Box, W. Barclay Craig and Harry Sullivan of M. Sullivan & Son Construction Company, met with Council explaining procedures taken to date and exhibited plans and specifications of the proposed hospital as drafted by Architects, Richards and Abra. At this meeting, Council introduced a by-law for the borrowing of $50,000 by debenture to remodel the McLachlin residence in keeping with hospital suitability. When the debenture by-law was presented to the people of Arnprior on December 6, 1943, the recorded vote was 562 in favor of the by-law and only 44 against.

The first Board of Directors elected on July 3, 1944 was composed of: Chairman, H. A. Short, Vice-Chairman, D. A. Gillies; Secretary, A. A. McLean; Treasurer, P. J. Lindsay; Directors elected for 3 years, H. A. Short, N. S. Robertson, C. A. Mulvihill, A. D. F. Campbell, D. A. Gillies; 2 years, R. A. Jeffery; W. A. Whyte, W. Barclay Craig, A. A. McLean, E. D. Osborne; one year, R. M.

Simpson, A. Steele Campbell, R. M. Neilson, E. Woermke, W. F. Hadley; Directors appointed, McNab Township, Milton Stewart; Fitzroy Township, Victor Major; Braeside, C. D. Young; Pakenham, R. M. Boal; Medical staff, Dr. J. Howard Box, Dr. A. H. Reid, J. P. Mulvihill.

The Civic Welfare Committee were very active in the fund raising campaign for necessary equipment and by June 1944 $52,797 had been subscribed. A Ladies Auxiliary was formed in 1961. Subsequent financial drives were always successful.

Through the generosity of Mrs. David A. Gillies, who donated the land, *"The Grove"* Nursing Home was opened in 1981 with a complement of 60 beds. This is under the jurisdiction of the Hospital Board.

It is interesting to note that the same spirit of the founders prevailed down through the years in the continuous operation of the hospital. It has been said the central theme of this motivation truly personified the *"Brotherhood of Man"*.

Some statistics relative to the hospital: The Arnprior & District Memorial Hospital, a 95 bed facility, provides 24 hour-a-day coverage for all patient care services. A doctor is on call each day to provide emergency room coverage and the X-ray, Laboratory and Operating Room staff also take daily calls.

The hospital maintains a full range of other services including ultrasonic examinations; electrocardiography; inhalation therapy; physiotherapy, medical, surgical, obstetri-

Arnprior and District Memorial Hospital, newer additions.

Photo by Hanson ©

Arnprior and District Memorial Hospital, original section.

The Grove Nursing Home.

cal, pediatric and chronic care wards; a 3 bed intensive care unit; out-patient day care services; activities program - chronic care; dietetic services and a *"meals on wheels"* program.

The Medical Staff is made up as follows:

Family Practice	- 10 active staff
	- 3 courtesy staff
	- 1 honorary staff
General Surgery	- 2 active staff
Consultants	- 4 honorary members
	- 4 active members
Dental Services	- 5 active staff
	- 1 active consultant
	- 1 courtesy staff

In keeping with the Board of Director's philosophy of a total health care concept, the Board undertook to build the Primary Health Care Centre in 1976, presently housing the offices of nine doctors, the Victorian Order of Nurses, a dentist and a denturist.

The Board of Directors 1983-1984 is as follows: President, Lt. Col. A. Gaumond; Vice-President, Mrs. M. Bews; Honorary Life Members, A. Steele Campbell, A. A. McLean; Elected Members, Mrs. M. Bews, Mrs. J.Clancy, Rev. R. J. Davis, Lt. Col. A. Gaumond, W. W. Gillespie, N. P. Hazelwood, L. D. Hill, Arthur McLean, H. A. Murdoch, F. A. Rosar, Mrs. M. Saunders, Nicholas Smith, M. T. Sullivan, T. E. Sullivan, I. Woermke. Appointed Members, Mrs. P. Camelon, Mrs. E. Delahunt, M. Smyth for Region of West Carleton; H. Barr, Township of Pakenham; W. F. Kauffeldt, Mrs. Patricia Robinson, Town of Arnprior; R. A. Stewart, Township of McNab; J. O. Smith, Braeside; Dr. D. D. Kearney, Dr. H. R. Giberson, Medical Staff; Mrs. K. Descent, Hospital Auxiliary.

ARNPRIOR MEDICAL CENTRE

THE ARNPRIOR Professional Holdings Limited Charter was issued July 23, 1956 to the following: Dr. H. R. Giberson, Dr. R. H. McCreary, J. J. Greene, C. S. Mulvihill, Catherine McNaughton. Directors were: Dr. J. H. Box, Dr. H. R. Giberson, Dr. R. H. McCreary, Dr. J. L. Dauphinais; Officers: President, Dr. J. H. Box; Vice-President, Dr. R. H. McCreary; Secretary-Treasurer, Dr. H. R. Giberson. On October 15, 1957, Dr. J. D. Bonell, being a shareholder of the Company by this time, was elected Director.

On May 3, 1956 the Company made an offer to purchase real estate on Daniel Street in the Town of Arnprior (i.e. part of lots 1 and 2 on said Daniel Street) with a Bruce G. Edward.

On October 15, 1957 it was resolved that the Company have authority to enter into a contract with M. Sullivan & Son Limited for the construction of a building on Daniel Street which would later be known as the Arnprior Medical Centre. The doctors moved into their new quarters on March 1, 1958.

Some further statistics: Dr. J. L. Dauphinais resigned as a Director, October 29, 1963; Dr. D. E. Box became a shareholder, October 29, 1963; Dr. D. E. Box resigned as Director, May 18, 1965; Dr. R. L. Roy was elected Director, May 18, 1965; Dr. A. G. Gregory became a shareholder, May 30, 1967; Dr. J. H. Box resigned, October 30, 1967; Dr. C. B. Cho-Chu became a shareholder, May 23, 1969.

It was on June 30, 1970, that Dr. R. H. McCreary retired from active practice at the Arnprior Medical Centre. Dr. McCreary was elected President of the Ontario Medical Association for the 1961-1962 term. He is the only physician in Eastern Ontario, outside of the cities of Ottawa and Kingston, to have occupied the prestigious office.

Arrivals: Dr. B. J. W. Cooper was in Arnprior from July 19, 1962 to July 1965; Dr. C. J. Parsons here from May 19, 1966 to June 1968; Dr. B. P. Persaud, July 11, 1968; Dr. D. D. Kearney, April 3, 1969; Dr. P. J. Ranson, July 1, 1970; Dr. Graham Morris, July 10, 1972; Dr. W. Earl Gordon, October 15, 1974; Dr. Brian Kelly, July 1, 1976; Dr. Mark Robson, May 19, 1981; and Dr. Grizel Amstee, July 4, 1983. The town also has five dental surgeons; Dr. W. Buttle, Dr. R. V. Glover, Dr. R. C. Whyte, Dr. P. A. Petryk and Dr. Patrick Heagney.

On March 1, 1977 the Arnprior Medical Centre moved to the Primary Health Care Centre, adjacent to the Arnprior & District Memorial Hospital.

The Medical Centre, or new Primary Health Care Centre, and its close proximity to the hospital, is not only beneficial to the doctors and staff but it greatly improves patient treatment as well. Many will recall the era when doctors practiced from their homes, made all sorts of sometimes unnecessary house calls and in all weather conditions.

The doctors of yesteryear set up a three room office in their homes consisting of a waiting room, a consulting room and the dispensary where the jingle of bottles meant some form of medicine was brewing. One such was a brown concoction smelling like creosote, and tasting as bad, but it cut a chest cold like a knife.

There is a parallel in some of the amusing pictures hanging in the consulting rooms of the medical centre with those on the walls of the doctor's office long ago. For instance, in Dr. W. B. McNaughton's Madawaska Street office, there was an eye catching, very thought provoking picture and poem. It depicted a *"smiling bum"* with all his tattered clothing and beneath the picture was inscribed this short verse:

"It's Easy Enough To Be Happy
When Life Goes Along Like a Song
But The Man Worthwhile Is The Man Who Can Smile
When Everything Goes Dead Wrong."

And in the new Primary Health Care Centre one will find some of Norman Rockwell's amusing caricatures like the little girl holding up her doll while a genial doctor checks the doll with a stethoscope and a young boy with his trousers down, standing on a chair, getting a needle shot in the rear.

ST. JOHN CHRYSOSTOM
ROMAN CATHOLIC CHURCH

THE FIRST Roman Catholic chapel in Arnprior was established in 1857 by Rev. Joseph Bouvier. Arnprior was expanding rapidly and Father Bouvier recognized the need for a new and larger Church. Sufficient land was donated by Daniel McLachlin and the chapel was enlarged temporarily in 1869. A new Church was begun in 1871 and completed in 1873 and the chapel transformed into a presbytery. The new Church was solemnly blessed and dedicated for Divine worship on August 5, 1874 under the title of St. John Chrysostom.

Rev. J. Alphonsus M. Chaine was appointed Parish Priest in 1875 at the age of 39 years and served in that

Original St. John Chrysostom Roman Catholic Church.

St. John Chrysostom Roman Catholic Church.

Photo courtesy Rev. D. Miller

Photo by Hanson

capacity for a record 41 years. Under Father Chaine's leadership the Parish flourished and a tremendous construction program emerged. In 1876 he built St. John Chrysostom Separate School and in 1885 the present brick rectory was built adjacent to the Church.

In keeping with the fast growing community, it became evident that a new and much larger Church was required and so Father Chaine began to make plans for the massive Gothic-style stone Church that was to become one of the finest and most beautiful structures dedicated to the greater Glory of God. Begun in 1904, the ceremony of the Blessing and laying of the cornerstone by Bishop N. Z. Lorrain, Bishop of Pembroke, took place July 1, 1907. The entire structure was sufficiently complete so that services could be held in the Church in 1908. The Church was built for $66,000 and contractors say it would cost at least $2 million to replace today. Subsequent Parish Priests were Monsignor Bernard J. Kiernan, 1916-1931; Monsignor Joseph T. Warnock, 1931-1954; Rev. John L. Enright, 1954-1956; Monsignor Reginald E. Dillon, 1956-1976. It was during Monsignor Dillon's pastorate that the Church was completely renovated and updated in accordance with Vatican II recommendations. Monsignor Dillon was also instrumental in the construction of the St. John Chrysostom Parish Hall. The next Pastor was Rev. Douglas J. Morris, 1976-1977. Because of ill health, Father Morris had to resign and take up duties in a small Parish at the time. Then followed Rev. R. Murray Tardiff, 1977-1982, during whose Pastorate the Parish experienced the most extensive and varied ministry program in its history. Father Tardiff resigned to become the Director of Chaplaincy Correctional Service of Canada.

The present Administrator is Rev. Daniel Miller, a young priest who served as Assistant to Father Tardiff and who is continuing the ministry program initiated by his predecessor.

ST. ANDREW'S PRESBYTERIAN CHURCH

IN 1859 DUE in no small measure to the labors of Dr. Alexander Mann, the Congregation of St. Andrew's was organized in connection with the Church of Scotland. There was no church building but much faith and hope and enthusiasm. In 1863 two streams of Presbyterianism came together. One had a minister but no church building. The other had a building but no minister. The result was inevitable. The augmented congregation flourished in it's new home at the corner of Albert and Ottawa Streets. There it was to worship for upwards of thirty years. Then under the leadership of Rev. D. J. McLean the St. Andrew's Congregation achieved maturity and strength. So much so that in 1890 the impressive stone church at the corner of Ottawa and John was built and dedicated and the congregation moved into it with rejoicing. In 1924 there came the vote on church union and with it the first chapter of St. Andrew's came to a close.

In 1925 those who decided to remain in the Presbyte-

rian Church in Canada found themselves without a church home. But what could measure the emotion and the dedication with which St. Andrew's reorganized itself on Easter Day that year? Courage ran high. Determination was unbounded. The vision of a new church rose in their minds like a star. Their numbers grew and their zeal was undiminished. In 1926 the Rev. E. J. Kerr was inducted. Under his leadership the dream came near fulfillment. The site was chosen. The plans ready. The foundation was prepared

St. Andrew's Presbyterian Church.

and the walls began to go up. What an uplifting of hearts: What a rich fellowship of work and shared hopes. Through storm and sun and tragedy the work went on until at last the house of their heart's desire stood there in all its beauty. On July 8, 1928 the Moderator of the General Assembly, the Rev. James Buchanan, D.D., officiated at the dedication of the present Church of St. Andrew's.

From 1928 the congregation in loyalty and happiness girded itself steadfastly to bear the inevitable and heavy burden of debt. Then the depression of the thirties rolling across the world came to the Ottawa Valley and to Arnprior. Dark indeed were those days for St. Andrew's. There were times when they were not sure if they could hold on to the church to which they had given so much of themselves. But miraculously and providentially, doors would open when all seemed closed and dark. After the War, St. Andrew's achieved status and became a self-sustaining charge. Organizations blossomed and church groups gained a new vitality. The difficult days were passed. In 1946 the mortgage was burned amidst general rejoicing and much celebration. In 1954 the Rev. Dr. C. J. St. Clair Jeans of Glasgow, Scotland, was inducted into St. Andrew's. In June of that year the new manse was started. Another venture recalling the enthusiasm and devotion of the old days.

The present minister, the Reverend Leo E. Hughes, was inducted on June 16, 1967. During the past 16 years St. Andrew's Place was purchased and extensive renovations made to the Church basement and kitchen. In 1976 the sanctuary was redecorated in preparation for the opening of the 102nd General Assembly of the Presbyterian Church in Canada. The General Assembly met in St. Andrew's from June 4 to 9 and brought together Commissioners from coast to coast to share in the hospitality of the Congregation. The Congregation received tremendous cooperation from the Arnprior Community and from sister Churches throughout the Presbytery.

"All this has been ours in the goodness and mercy of a loving God. How else could we have done it? In humble thankfulness we confront the next fifty years in confidence that He, who has done so marvellously in our past, will show us and ours, in the years to be, greater things out of His storehouse."

WESLEYAN CHURCH

IT WAS about 1875 that the Zion Evangelical congregation purchased the former frame-constructed, white-painted church on Harrington Street which had been the local Methodist Church. The purchase occurred when the Methodist congregation built a new brick edifice on John Street, presently Grace-St. Andrew's Christian Education Centre.

About 1909, during the Pastorate of Rev. Orlando G. Hallman, the frame church was demolished and the present brick structure was built. A devout member of the church, Mrs. Frank Boese, at age 91, the oldest living member, likes to reminisce on the early days of the church. The beginnings of the then Zion Evangelical Church go back to the 1870's when many German people left their homeland to settle in Canada. Mrs. Boese' parents, Mr. and Mrs. August Albert Heise, emigrated from Germany in 1887. A brother of Mrs. Boese became an Evangelical minister.

The original Zion Evangelical Church of the 1870's has undergone several name revisions since that era. In the early 1900's it became the Evangelical United Brethren Church and still later it became the Wesleyan Methodist Church. It is now the Wesleyan Church and a new minister in the person of Rev. Robert Joseph Hooper has recently been appointed Pastor. The Wesleyan Women's Missionary Society is quite prominent in the activities of the church.

GRACE-ST. ANDREW'S UNITED CHURCH

A RICH HERITAGE surrounds Grace-St. Andrew's United Church in Arnprior. Known as the *"Stone Church"* at the turn of the century, Grace-St. Andrew's is a unique blend of Gothic and Victorian styling, featuring buttresses that suggest strength and support. Like so many other churches of its day, the church faces to the east and thus symbolizes Christ as *"The Sun of the Universe in its rising"*.

Less obvious to the casual observer, Grace-St. Andrew's exemplified harmony; in 1925, when the Church Union united the Methodist, Presbyterian and Congregational churches in Canada, the Grace (Methodist) and St. Andrew's (Presbyterian) churches combined to form what is now known as the Grace-St. Andrew's United Church. This auspicious union took place on June 10. But what of the beginnings of these two churches?

Many of the first settlers who arrived in Arnprior around 1840 were Presbyterian, either belonging to the United Presbyterian or Old Kirk bodies. The congregation of St. Andrew's Church was organized in 1859, followed by organization of the Wesleyan Methodists in 1863. The Methodist circuit became known as the Pakenham and Arnprior Mission. The original frame church was eventually replaced about 1881 by a brick building on John Street. In 1894, the congregation erected a greatly enlarged edifice known as Grace Church, which now serves as a Parish Hall for Christian Education purposes. As Arnprior grew and prospered — and once the Presbyterian groups had united — the Presbyterians wanted to erect a new structure. Under Rev. D. J. McLean's ministry, which began in 1871 and lasted 35 years, the ground for the new *"Stone Church"* was broken on July 1, 1890. On August 27, the cornerstone was laid by Mrs. Daniel McLachlin of the McLachlin Lumbering empire. The cost of construction was $17,812.

Since the union in 1925, the congregation has chosen to worship in the *"Stone Church"* which has undergone several refurbishments since. In 1967, the entrance and

Wesleyan Church

Photo by Hanson

interior were redesigned: a new Casavant pipe organ was installed at a cost of $25,700; new furniture was installed throughout the sanctuary; and a new basement complete with meeting rooms, Chapel, infant nursery and modern church offices was finished.

Under the supervision of its latest minister, the Rev. Ross Davis, these basement rooms are once again being refurbished. Many of the older prints found in closets or donated by members of the congregation, along with framed photographs of the church's earlier ministers, have been hung — to serve as constant reminders that Grace-St. Andrew's United Church is alive, thanks to its solid foundation.

EMMANUEL ANGLICAN CHURCH

THE LAND for Emmanuel Anglican Church was given by Daniel McLachlin and the church was built in 1869. Before this, monthly services were held in the area by the Rector of Fitzroy Harbour. The Rev. C. T. Denroche built the church and rectory in 1869. Between 1884 and 1886 the Chancel was built; also the vestry and tower and, very importantly in our climate, a furnace was installed.

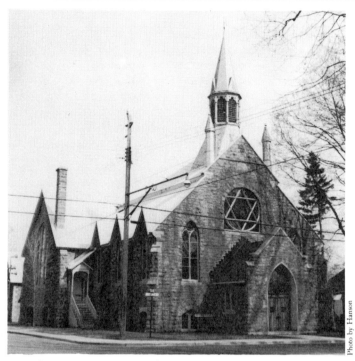

Grace-St. Andrew's United Church

Photo by Hanson

Emmanuel Anglican Church 1900

Photo courtesy Jean Macnamara Cunningham

Among the later Rectors of the Parish were: the Rev. R. G. Fiander; the late Harry Hobbs, Dean of Brandon; the Rev. Alan Meakin; the Rev. Allan Box; and the present rector is the Rev. Archie Hunter.

In 1962 a dream was realized when the Parish Hall, named in memory of the late Carlton Reid, was completed to mark the 100th Anniversary of the Parish.

In 1966 a Parish Council was formed which directs the various aspects of parish life. Over the years there have been active Women's groups in the Parish, originally a Parish Guild and the Women's Auxiliary and in 1974, in conjunction with the National church, the groups amalgamated and became Anglican Church Women. There have been girls and Junior Auxiliaries and branches of the Anglican Young People's Association. The church school has carried on over the years with a good attendance. More recently Pastoral care and Outreach groups have been formed with active programs being carried out. Many of those of the Outreach group are ecumenical.

Emmanuel Anglican Church 1908

The Parish has tried over the years to meet the social and spiritual needs of the parishioners that they may grow in Faith and in the Christian life and to live the meaning of the church's name, Emmanuel, which translated is *"God With Us"*.

FIRST BAPTIST CHURCH

THE EARLY records of the First Baptist Church have been lost but from the Annual Year Books and publications of the Eastern Conference of the North American Baptist Convention, references indicate the church was established in 1869. The first recorded minutes of the church's possession are written in German script and dated May 7, 1873.

Rev. G. A. Schulte, the first General Missionary Secretary of the Triennial Conference, in his book, *"Reminiscences of my Fifty Years Missionary Services"*, mentions a visit he made to Arnprior and Sebastopol about 1871 and then he found German Baptists in Arnprior and about five miles west of Arnprior in McNab Township.

First Baptist Church

The first resident Pastor was Rev. J. J. Valkenaar who served from 1873 to 1879.

It was in 1872 that a section of land in the northwest corner of the Eric Harrington farm was purchased and the church edifice erected in the same year, which still serves the congregation. It was remodelled in 1926 during the pastorate of Rev. Francis L. Strobel. A few years after construction of the church, a log house was built on the same lot to serve as a residence for the Pastors. A new manse was erected on the Alicia Street property in 1956. Some of the pioneers appearing in early records are the Dieners, Scheels, Runtz, Streich, Redtmann, Berndt, Nieman, Jahnke, Duemmel and Schlacter.

The first major renovations were made to the original church during the pastorate of Rev. Strobel 1924-1929. It was in 1956, during the pastorate of Rev. Walter Schmidt, that a new Parsonage was built.

Under the leadership of Rev. Loren A. Weber, a new Building Committee was appointed with Gerald Kuehl as Chairman. An extensive remodelling program was launched; a new front addition extending across the width of the church was built, with the new entrance facing Alicia Street. An enlarged lobby was provided on the main floor. The second floor includes a nursery and washrooms and the basement area provides a lower level lobby with increased washroom and storage facilities. The basement area now includes seven classrooms and with the installation of folding doors it was designed as a flexible unit adaptable to large group assemblies. A new heating system was installed as well as improved kitchen facilities. The sanctuary was re-modelled and the Chancel area re-designed.

The last two pastors were Rev. Kenneth MacDonald and Rev. David Glader. At the time of writing the church is being served by an interim pastor.

PENTECOSTAL GLAD TIDINGS CHURCH

IT WAS in April 1918 that Rev. George Chambers, a Pentecostal minister from Ottawa, came to Arnprior and conducted meetings in the Town Hall. Large crowds attended and it was decided to build a church on Victoria Street on a property donated by James Fraser. The church was built by John Runtz and officially opened in November 1920 with the Rev. G. A. Chambers as the first minister.

The congregation increased over the years and in 1962 a large extension was added with a new educational wing to accommodate the large Sunday School classes.

Rev. William Kenna is the 22nd pastor. He succeeded Rev. Les Grant in September 1983.

Anniversary services celebrating 65 years of ministry to the community of Arnprior and district were held in November 1983.

Pentecostal Church

ST. JOHN'S EVANGELICAL LUTHERAN CHURCH

DURING THE 1880's there was considerable immigration to this area from Germany. Some were attracted by the opportunity for farming, others by the opportunity for immediate employment in the lumber industry where there was a constant demand for unskilled labor in the sawmills and in the lumber yard during the summer and in the logging camps during the winter. These people soon established homes for themselves both in town and also the surrounding suburbs.

Some of these immigrants were of the Lutheran denomination and their spiritual needs were cared for by the occasional visit of a Lutheran missionary with services conducted in homes. However, they soon wished for regular services. In 1889 under the guidance of the Rev. G. Brackebusch, then a missionary to the area, a congregation was constitutionally organized with the name of The Evangelical Lutheran Saint John's Congregation. The same year a building site was purchased from Eric Harrington at the corner of McLachlin and Alicia Streets. Construction was begun and the church completed during 1890 and dedicated on January 18, 1891. Though very modest in size, nevertheless it was built in the very architectural style of many small churches in the villages of northern Germany. They would be built of brick or stone, while here it was a wood frame structure since lumber was readily available at reasonable cost.

St. John Evangelical Lutheran Church 1889

The church had an octagonal Chancel with the Altar at its centre. It was an ornate, admirable piece of workmanship with its high Gothic-type reredos and matching communion rail. There was a very high pulpit standing on its pedestal of columns and a narrow staircase ascending to it.

At the back there was a small gallery or choir loft with a pedal pump reed organ.

St. John Evangelical Lutheran Church

During the winter the church was heated by a huge cast-iron, wood-burning stove which consumed large two-foot blocks of cord wood. Though there was a good stone foundation supporting the walls, there was no basement; it was considered unnecessary. The exterior walls were sheathed with "V" joint white pine clapboards and painted white with the result it became known and spoken of as *"The Little White Church"* for many years.

In 1948 the church was rebuilt. The frame shell of the original building was half-turned and placed on new concrete walls of a full sized basement. This was necessary so that a new and larger Chancel could be added.

The new basement housed rooms for the Sunday school, kitchen, furnace room and washrooms. A new and larger narthex was added, topped by a spire and belfry in which a few years later a chime of three bells was placed. The exterior walls were housed in with brick giving the building a more substantial appearance.

Some years later the old reed organ was discarded and a good pipe organ was installed.

In 1970 there was a further renovation of the interior in a more modern and contemporary design.

ELGIN STREET BAPTIST CHURCH

ORGANIZED BAPTIST work began in Ottawa in 1857 but it was some years later that churches began to appear in the upper Ottawa Valley. Who began the work in the Arnprior district is not known. However, the records show that on December 24, 1874 the Regular Baptist Church of Arnprior was organized with fifteen charter members.

A few years previous to this, in 1869, a group of German immigrants who were Baptists had formed a small German Baptist Church. They constructed the brick building in the southwest part of the village now known as First Baptist Church. Arrangements were made whereby the newly-formed English congregation was allowed to use the building to conduct one service each Sunday. The arrangement continued until the English group built the brick church on Elgin Street which is presently used.

Elgin Street Baptist Church

Some of the names appearing in the early minutes of the church are: McDonald, Macnab, Farmer, Kerr, Sheffield, Parsons, Grierson, Robinson, Cram and Moore.

Some of these families are still represented in the membership of the church. The land for the church was purchased in 1891 and early in 1902 building operations commenced. The building committee consisted of William Farmer, Archie Kerr, G. F. Macnab, J. G. Ledgerwood, George Sheffield, G. W. Rudlen and John Grierson. The contractor was S. R. Rudd and W. I. Parsons was superintendent of construction. The cornerstone was laid in 1902 by Mrs. Robert McDonald. Dedication services were held on Sunday, January 11, 1903 with pastor, Rev. M. C. McLean and Rev. J. L. Gilmour, pastor of Olivet Baptist Church, Montreal, as guest speaker for the occasion.

On March 6, 1949 a disastrous fire occurred in the church building and extensive renovations had to be conducted throughout the structure. Again in 1958-59 further improvements were made in the basement of the church; the kitchen was modernized and unused space converted into a vestry room and a ladies' parlor with the latter furnished by special donations given in memory of Jean Sheffied who had been church organist for over forty years. The room is known as *"The Sheffield Room"*.

The church has an active Sunday School organization. With regard to Women's Organizations, it is not known just when the first women's organizations were formed in the church but from 1906 on there are references in the minutes to the Ladies' Aid and the Women's Mission Circle. About 1920 a Young Women's Mission Circle was organized.

On June 19, 1969, the White Lake Baptist Church joined with the Elgin Street Church in Arnprior. The present Minister is the Rev. R. Simmons.

CALVARY BAPTIST CHURCH

SUNDAY, NOVEMBER 28, 1965, was an important day in the lives of the congregation of Calvary Baptist Church, for on that day Pastor R. A. Baker turned the first sod at the site of what was to be a very impressive edifice, the new Calvary Baptist Church on the corner of Edey and Landrigan Streets. Speaking to the gathering, Pastor Baker quoted the psalmist, *"Except the Lord build the house they labor in vain that built it"*. Prominent church layman, Deacon Ellwood S. McCrea, spoke briefly prior to the symbolic ceremony. Members of the church building committee were: William Slater, Donald Glenn, Donald Slater, Emerson Scheel, Fred Scheel, Ellwood McCrea and Walter Slater.

Photo by Hanson

Calvary Baptist Church

And another glorious day in the life of Calvary Baptist was Sunday, May 7, 1978, when the congregation took part in the Mortgage Burning ceremony.

The Calvary Baptist in Arnprior came into being in June 1940 when services were held in homes of the members. The first Pastor was Rev. Brynle Owens whose years of ministry until 1957 were, in the words of Deacon McCrea, *"ones of pastoral sacrifice and inspiring leadership"*. Premises were rented at 56 Madawaska Street and the property was finally purchased in 1945.

Following a period of supply Pastors, the Rev. Neil D. Beattie came to Arnprior in 1959 and in his two year pastorate the property on Edey Street was purchased. Subsequent Pastors were, Rev. D. C. Harry, Rev. M. J.

Gibson, Rev. Robert Baker, Rev. John Jones and Rev. M. Hollywood. The present Pastor is Rev. John Roberts. It was during Pastor Baker's pastorate that the decision to proceed with construction of the new church was arrived at.

The Board of Deacons at the time was composed of William Slater, Chairman; Don Slater, Don Glenn and Ellwood McCrea. Of interest is that the 1940 Board consisted of Chairman George Bond, Walter Slater, Emerson Scheel and Ellwood McCrea.

The Ladies' Dorcas Society of the Church is prominent in Church affairs along with many of the younger people.

Built by General Contractor Don Sullivan, the main body of the Church is 60 feet long by 32 feet wide, with 23 twelve foot pews that can accommodate 161 persons. The roof is supported by six laminated arches; windows have panels of green and amber cathedral glass. In the sanctuary three rows of pews flank out on both sides to doorways. The baptistry surmounts the sanctuary. The basement area contains the Church Hall which measures 50 feet by 23 feet; a nursery room; Sunday School office; several utility rooms; rest rooms; a modern kitchen and storage space.

On Sunday May 15, 1966, the official dedication ceremonies took place with Rev. M. J. Gibson, a former Pastor, guest speaker for the occasion and Pastor R. A. Baker in charge of ceremonies.

GOSPEL HALL

IT WAS IN 1929 that Evangelist R. J. Brooks came to Arnprior and founded the Gospel Hall congregation, a group of Christian believers that have expanded throughout the years.

The first services were held in a large tent located on McGonigal Street. Church services were also conducted in

Photo courtesy A. T. "Sandy" Campbell

Gospel Hall

private homes for a while with lay ministers leading the congregation.

Prior to 1950, church services were held in a building on Elgin Street East and later the congregation occupied an upper hall located on John Street.

In the Autumn of 1950, the elders and the congregation acquired land on William Street where they decided to build the present attractive Gospel Hall. The building was completed early in 1951 with the congregation occupying the new church in February of that year.

Of staunch Christian principles, the Gospel Hall congregation have, in recent years, commended to the Mission Field, three full-time workers; this in addition to four young people to short-term Missionary work consisting of from one to two years duration. To date, one Missionary, Beverley Boyle, is working full time in Spain. Another, Arthur Raddatz, son of Mr. and Mrs. Emerson Raddatz, was killed in an accident during his term as a Missionary in the Dominican Republic, and a sister, Elaine Raddatz of Toronto, has also served in the Mission Field.

Another young lay Minister, David Campbell, son of Mr. and Mrs. A. T. "Sandy" Campbell, served four years in South Korea and is presently in Alberta where he also participates in the lay ministry work.

Among the Gospel Hall high priorities is the worship of God; to share in fellowship; and to give the good news of the Gospel to the World.

JEHOVAH'S WITNESSES

IN THE early 1950's some Jehovah's Witnesses from the Renfrew congregation visited homes in the Arnprior area and Bible meetings were held in a private home. In 1957 two special representatives were sent to Arnprior and in a short time a few people showed interest and a congregation was formed.

In 1958 an invitation went out to all congregations in Canada for individuals and families to move to areas like Arnprior, there to assist and encourage existing assemblies. Subsequent meetings were held in a room above the old

Kingdom Hall, Jehovah's Witnesses

Beamish store on John Street and later to a basement location in a private home.

Towards the end of 1960, it became apparent that a larger, more permanent meeting place was needed. A property on Second Avenue was purchased and a Kingdom Hall, large enough to seat 100 persons, was built by volunteer workers. Today, close to one hundred people attend the Sunday meetings; five ministers oversee the congregation and 55 participate in the door-to-door preaching work on a regular basis.

ARNPRIOR'S NEWSPAPERS

THE TOWN of Arnprior might well boast that it has had some of the finest weekly publications in the country down through the years. Newspaper printing has come a long way since the day of the horse-operated treadmill that supplied power for the presses. Prior to the 1950's there were few technological changes in newspaper weeklies and the Linotype was the most important. That so-called *"mechanical wizard"* freed the printer from the type case where it was necessary to pick up each letter of every word from a cupboard drawer and place it in the proper location for the press. Then the type had to be put back in the drawer until the next week. In the 1960's came the offset presses. Today, for instance, the Arnprior Chronicle is set on discs, fed into computers, photographed and printed on a large offset press that does the job much faster. Arnprior's second newspaper, the Arnprior Guide, is an exceptionally highly computerized system.

THE STAR AND
THE ARNPRIOR WEEKLY REVIEW

PERHAPS THE earliest newspaper published in the then village of Arnprior, The Star, was actually a daily. Published in the late 1860's, The Star had a circulation between 800 to 1,000 copies per day. It was delivered throughout the community for five cents per week; the price for a single copy was one cent; price per year $2.50. The publisher was J. H. Nicholson and the office was located at 26 Elgin Street. It is thought the publication ceased during the 1870's.

The Arnprior Weekly Review was being published in 1873, followed by the semi-weekly News. Very little is known of these publications.

THE ARNPRIOR CHRONICLE

ESTABLISHED BY Munn & MacDonald in 1879 from a location on Madawaska Street and later in the Phoenix Block, John Street, the Chronicle celebrated the 100th Anniversary of its founding a few years ago. Still recognized as one of the outstanding weeklies in the country, the Chronicle, almost every year, has won numerous awards in various classifications as judged by the Ontario Weekly Newspaper Association. The newspaper was sold in 1905 to A. J. Jeffery and later his son R. A. Jeffery assumed control and remained publisher until November 1929, when he sold it to W. H. McFarlane, the former owner of The Lanark Era. In June 1951, McFarlane sold The Chronicle to R. S. Atkey who published the newspaper through the 1950's and early 1960's. In February 1965 The Chronicle was purchased by County Newspapers Limited, a division of Thomson newspapers. Donald W. McCuaig of Renfrew then purchased The Chronicle in May 1975 and it became part of a chain which included the Renfrew Mercury and the Carleton Place Canadian.

It was on October 5, 1978 that The Chronicle, along with its sister papers, were purchased by the present publisher, Donald F. Runge and became part of Runge Newspapers Incorporated, with his son Fred as General Manager of the chain, which now includes the Almonte Gazette and the Pembroke Advertiser News. The Chronicle also incorporates a West Carleton Banner supplement.

THE ARNPRIOR WATCHMAN

FIRST ORGANIZED in March 1880 by E. K. Johnston, The Watchman was published from an office located in the burned out Beamish Block. In the early days The Watchman was literally a *"one horsepower"* operation — the printing press was operated by a sort of treadmill powered by a single horse. The horse, walking nowhere, on the escalator-like treadmill, located in the yard behind the printing office, treaded the endless belt providing the power to work the printing press.

The paper was purchased by J. C. Williams, father of Mrs. Edith Osborne, in 1898. Following the death of Williams in 1916, the newspaper was sold to A. E. Bradwin who operated it until it ceased publication in 1920.

The prohibition vote of January 1894 resulted in Arnprior voting in favor of prohibition. The poll was 213 For, while 199 voted Against prohibition. The Watchman published at that time by Johnston, apparently was strongly in favor of prohibition because the paper published several indicative comments on the result of the vote, one of which was, *"only a few insignificant towns and villages in the whole province decided in favor of whiskey"*.

THE DEUTSCHE POST

THE DEUTSCHE Post was published in Arnprior by E. B. Christiansen, a one-time Lutheran pastor who after retiring from the ministry also organized and managed the newspaper. It was published about 1904 until 1910 in an office on Madawaska Street. In the early 1900's Arnprior and the surrounding district had a fairly large German population and the Deutsche Post was quite popular and had a good circulation. Besides a large percentage of citizens of German origin in Arnprior itself, the population in Mansfield was about 75 percent German extraction, while the 9th and 10th concessions of McNab Township were then known as the *"German Settlement"*.

Christiansen later moved to Pembroke where he re-established the Deutsche Post. Following his death, a son Emile, took over the business, discontinued the newspaper but expanded in the printing field.

Of local interest is, that it was with Emile Christiansen in Pembroke that the Runge brothers, Walter, Fred and Max, learned the printing business. The brothers later moved to Ottawa where Fred and Max organized and operated the Runge Brothers Printing in 1912, later known as the Runge Press. The senior Fred is the father of Donald F. Runge who purchased a printing and stationery business in Pembroke in 1957 and who is now the publisher of the Runge Newspapers Incorporated under which The Chronicle is published.

THE ARNPRIOR GUIDE

THE ARNPRIOR Guide was founded by Steve Prensler, a native of Arnprior. As a young boy, Prensler served his printing apprenticeship both with J. C. Williams, Publisher of The Watchman and with R. A. Jeffery, Publisher of The Chronicle.

Following a two year stint with Hanson & Edgar at Kingston, he opened his own job printing shop on Elgin Street and later purchased the building on John Street where he ultimately founded The Guide, first known as The Shopper's Guide. In addition to a large job printing business and the publication of The Guide, Steve and his wife Blanche *"Bud"* Prensler, handled the Motor Vehicle Licence Bureau from 1939 until 1965. They sold the business and building to G. S. Levy in March 1965. In 1966 Levy sold the business to Gordon Fenn and it was in 1977 that Fenn's daughter Sue and her husband Derek Walters assumed control of the business. The Arnprior Guide is presently a highly computerized newspaper. Sue Walters tells of how this came about. While involved in church work the Walters met with Mr. and Mrs. Farrell Chown of Mohr's Corners, Galetta. Chown had been associated with the Fitzmohr Associates Computer Company and had retired early. He proferred technical advice and designed a program which was adopted by the newspaper. So successful was the program that representatives of the Post Office Department were interested and brought in people to look at the newspaper computer setup.

DIAMOND PARK SPRINGS

FOUNDED BY John A. MacDonald, one-time publisher of The Chronicle, somewhere between 1890 and 1896, Diamond Park Springs has a certain place in the history of Arnprior. The Spring, now flooded by Ontario Hydro in the construction of the new dam and generating station resulting in the creation of Lake Madawaska, was located at the western extremity of Pakenham Township just below the Tom Havey farm. It was about 100 yards from the river bank and flowed at the rate of ten gallons per minute.

Diamond Park Mineral Water became world famous. Among the components were salt and sulphur and the water was said to have curative powers dealing with rheumatic problems, hangover headaches, and an aid in flushing the kidneys. A plant employing about twelve people was constructed. The mineral water was bottled in quarts, pints and half pints and packed in wooden cases for shipment throughout the world.

A frame hotel comprising some twelve rooms with a verandah fronting the river, was built and proved a popular *"spa"* during summer months. The hotel was destroyed by fire in 1909.

The plant was eventually sold to Sanitaris Limited who continued bottling the mineral water in their building, presently occupied by Isolation Systems Limited. Sanitaris is a derivative of the words *"sanitary"* and *"Appolonaris"*, a world famous product at that time. Sanitaris also bottled fresh water from McLachlin's South Yard spring. At one time when a typhoid epidemic threatened the city of Ottawa, Sanitaris shipped, every week to that city, a carload of the fresh Spring water bottled in five gallon containers. Sanitaris also manufactured some soda pop drinks before closing permanently.

ARNPRIOR BOTTLING WORKS

ANOTHER MANUFACTURER of soft drinks was the Arnprior Bottling Works owned and operated by D. K. Cunningham about 1910. The plant, situated on the corner of Elgin and Russell Streets, was of frame construction with metal siding. They manufactured popular soft drinks of the time including ginger ale, iron brew, cream soda, birch beer, orange sparkle and lemon sour.

The trademark on the bottles was a *"bell"*. Benny Friday, native of Arnprior and an authority on bygone days, has one of the *"bell"* bottles in his possession. An apparatus converted the town's water pressure into sufficient power to operate the brushes used in bottle washing as well as the foot-pedal operated bottle capping machine.

ARNPRIOR'S HOTELS

ARNPRIOR NEVER got its *"Del Prado"* hotel, mooted back in 1914 to be the *"Chateau Laurier"* of Arnprior, but the town did boast seven hotels at one time from the 1875 era on into the 1900's.

The much talked of *"Del Prado"* was to replace the *"Grand Union"* hotel located on the southwest corner of John and Elgin Streets, now the Caruso block. It was designed by Ottawa architect Francis C. Sullivan and in July 1914 construction was all set to go. But, according to a qualified source, the First Great War put a stop to everything and the dream never materialized.

Back in the days when Arnprior's main streets were a sea of mud and/or dust, hotels with their accompanying bars, played a big part in the development of the town.

THE LYONS HOTEL

The Lyons Hotel on the corner of Hugh (now Bell) and Madawaska Streets, the site of the present Madawaska Hotel, was the first such in the then village of Arnprior. Of frame construction, the building fronted on Madawaska Street. A wide doorway with fan lights above, entered into a hallway and the lobby. The dining room was situated on the left and the bar located on the right. The bar was built of heavy hardwood, highly polished, with a brass footrail.

Cuspidors were spotted here and there to catch the tobacco juice which the lumbermen aimed from a distance of six or more feet. A big yard, with stables, was located just off Hugh Street and the hotel was a favorite *"stopping"* place during the winter for Pontiac farmers hauling wood across Chats Lake. The rooms were located on the second floor.

The most pretentious hotels of the time were the famed Campbell House and the McPhee House (later the New Byrne and now the Cameron Hotel).

THE CAMPBELL HOUSE

The Campbell House complex was the biggest hotel ever in Arnprior. Built and operated by Archie Campbell, the main building was a three storey frame structure on the corner of John and Elgin Streets now the site of the Moskos Block. The hotel fronted on Elgin Street with a double verandah; captain's chairs, where the *"Town Wits"* voiced their words of wisdom, were numerous and these were placed along platforms fronting both Elgin and John Streets. Leading from the main entrance there was a wide staircase. The polished hardwood bar was a thing of class, built just high enough so that the clientele could rest elbows on the top while placing a foot on the bright brass rail below. A full length bar mirror faced the patrons and there was an impressive array of whiskey bottles and glasses in front of the mirror. The dining room was facing John Street. In those early days commercial travellers were high class patrons for the hotelier and competition for this type of clientele was keen. The travellers, referred to as *"drummers"*, would bring in trunkloads of merchandise, remaining at the hotel for several days, displaying their products to local merchants who would place orders at this time. So the smart hotel owner provided *"sample"* rooms for use by the traveller in displaying his wares. The Campbell House had several of these.

So important were those periodic visits by the salesmen that the firm of E. D. Osborne & Son had three floors of merchandise using a *"rope and pulley"* operated elevator to carry the stuff to the top floors.

The Campbell House as well as the McPhee House, operated a horse-drawn bus service to meet all passenger trains (in those days there were ten trains each day) and pick up the commercial traveller and transport his cases to and from the hotel. The railways also sold special Commercial Traveller tickets at reduced rates.

On the Elgin Street side of the Campbell House there was a large gateway leading to a big hotel yard and stables.

There was a door from the bar to the yard; a door often used by "bouncers" who kept order in the hotel and literally heaved the belligerent drunk through the doorway. Fistfights in and around the hotel and yards were not uncommon during that era.

A feature of the Campbell House yard was a sawlog wooden pump. The apparatus above the "well" consisted of a five foot log with a fourteen inch diameter hole bored through its length. There was a wooden handle on the pump with a wood or iron spigot attached. This "well" was said to boast the finest drinking water in town. There were also facilities for watering horses.

The hotel yard separated the hotel proper from part of its complex that included several sample rooms, Kittner's Barber shop, Crown Lands office, Galvin's Tailor shop and other offices, all on the Elgin Street side.

THE MCPHEE HOUSE

The McPhee House was a very "swank" hotel competing with the Campbell House for top honors in the business. Of brick construction, the McPhee House was built on the corner of John and McGonigal Streets with the front off John Street. There was a verandah across the front and also along McGonigal Street and, of course, the Captain's chairs were prominent along these portions. The three storey structure had a large lobby off the main entrance with the stairway in its present location. The dining room was on the left with the kitchen in the rear. The fashionably elegant bar with its large mirror and brass rails was on the right of the lobby; draft beer was in barrels downstairs and piped up under its own pressure and through spigots beneath the bar. It is said that when the foam had settled, a drinker's glass would be only half full and he would push it back to the bartender saying, "put a little more foam on it".

A large yard with stables was at the back of the lot with entrances off both John and McGonigal Streets. Six sample rooms were located in the building to the north side of the yard. Like the Campbell House, the McPhee operated a horse-drawn vehicle to and from all passenger trains. This bus could accommodate about ten people, had steel rimmed wooden wheels with springs, with a canopy of wood and canvas and canvas sides if weather was inclement.

THE KING EDWARD HOTEL

The King Edward Hotel, boasting a striking name, was located on the northeast side of Elgin and Daniel Streets. The main building was a three storey brick structure with the main entrance off Elgin Street. The Daniel Street side, containing kitchens, was two-storey in height. From the main entrance one entered the lobby. The bar was on the right but was not so ornate as those of the two major hotels but nonetheless popular. The hotel dining room was on the left. The hotel yard entrance and stables was off Elgin Street.

THE O'NEILL HOUSE

The O'Neill House was on the southeast corner of Elgin and Daniel Streets; a two storey frame construction with the entrance off Elgin Street to the lobby. The bar was on the left of the lobby with the dining room and kitchen to the right. The O'Neill House was particularly popular with area farmers during the winter. They would haul wood to the hotel yard, stable the horses, and sell wood to local people who would call at the familiar wood-yard market.

THE GRAND UNION HOTEL

The Grand Union Hotel on the southwest corner of John and Elgin Streets was also a "class" hotel of the day. The main entrance was off Elgin Street; the lobby on the left; the bar on the right and the dining room and kitchen at the rear of the main floor.

MCGREGOR'S HOTEL

McGregor's Hotel, a small frame and stucco two-storey building, was on Elgin Street, the present site of the Giant Tiger business. The doorway was off Elgin to the lobby with the bar directly behind. As usual, the place had a street level platform with the customary Captain's chairs.

In addition to the seven hotels with their "booze" outlets, there were also two liquor stores; John Cunningham, grandfather of John and Jim McGonigal, had a liquor store next to his grocery business on Elgin Street. Cunningham owned a large business block from the corner of Elgin and Harriet Streets extending east on Elgin to the Drysdale Block. The second liquor outlet was that of Mort Sullivan on Madawaska Street.

THEATRE AND STAGE

THE FATHER of motion pictures in Arnprior was John S. Phillips. The first theatre, the Theatorium, was built in 1906 on the site of the present O'Brien Theatre by Phillips.

During the years 1904-1905, Phillips crossed the continent showing motion pictures with a bioscope, then considered a wonder machine. Crowded houses greeted Phillips in every town and city and in the majority of these, motion pictures had been discussed and talked of but never seen. Realizing the possibilities, Phillips returned to Arnprior and built the Theatorium. His theatre staff consisted of A. L. Johnston, Operator; J. P. Dontigny, soloist; Eva Young, cashier; Phillip Dontigny Jr., pianist; and Oscar Caillier and L. J. Kennedy, ushers.

That was the era when illustrated songs were a feature of every program. Western thrillers were a part of all programs and there was a liberal number of vaudeville numbers.

In 1908 Murtagh Sullivan and John Lumsden took a flyer in the motion picture game. They erected a tent on Elgin Street between John and Daniel Streets. It was quickly purchased by Phillips but this phase of his operation was doomed — a strong wind storm demolished the tent and Phillips sold the equipment.

A few years later, Guli Lodge and James Wallace built the Family Theatre on the same site as formerly occupied by the tent theatre. After about a year Phillips purchased this theatre also. This building also came to grief when a heavy fall of snow caved in the roof.

In April 1913, Phillips disposed of the Theatorium and the equipment of the Family Theatre to Herb Jordan and Syd Jennings of Renfrew and shortly thereafter their control was assumed by the O'Brien interests. The Theatorium and other Valley houses were operated by the Ottawa Valley Amusement Company until 1919 when the Casino Theatre was built by M. Sullivan & Son for the Ottawa Valley Amusement Company.

With the advent of talking pictures, the O'Brien people completely renovated and refurnished the old Casino Theatre and named it the O'Brien Theatre.

Throughout the history of motion pictures in Arnprior, two names stand out, those of John S. Phillips and J. P. Dontigny. The former brought the movies to Arnprior and during his regime gave the public the best releases obtainable, all at a price of five and ten cents. Assisting in making the Theatorium a popular house was J. P. Dontigny, for many years manager of the Casino Theatre.

The long deserted but memory laden *"third floor"* in Arnprior's historic Town Hall is a thing of the past but it is not forgotten. The *"show biz"* era in the Town Hall was abandoned many years ago. In a move with a two-fold purpose, namely, to make necessary renovations and at the same time modernize the old structure so as to provide facilities in keeping with a conventional municipal hall, the original roof was replaced; the giant British Columbia fir open beam structure was removed; the balcony taken out; and now the *"third floor"* is made up of well designed municipal offices and storage place.

Prior to the renovation program, the historic *"third floor"*, once the scene of many glittering performances by the renowned Marks Brothers Vaudeville troupe, minstrel groups and other professional productions, as well as hundreds of amateur plays and musical performances by local and Ottawa Valley theatre organizations, had slipped into a dismal, cold, tomb-like atmosphere.

The *"third floor"* was equipped with an orchestra platform, a once modern stage replete with appropriate backdrop scenery of the period, a spacious balcony that together with the main hall could seat 600 people. Some great character actors and musicians were developed locally and played to packed houses. Among those were Joe Murphy, remembered as one of the greatest *"ad libbers"* in amateur theatre, R. A. Jeffery who possessed the ability to be one of the best minstrel show interlocutors, Leo O'Neill, George Valin, Mamie Dontigny, Kathleen Murphy, Kathleen Hornidge, Sid Galvin, Cloud Tierney, Blanche *"Bud"* Prensler, Florence Otterson Nicholas and Jim Mulvihill. Among the noted soloists were Nellie Meek and Doris Byrne Mulvihill. Noted pianists were Frances Murphy and Nora O'Connor. Orchestra members of the era included Lillian Lindsay, Dan O'Connor and F. X. Desarmia, all violin specialists, and Edgar *"Tid"* Dontigny who could make the drums talk.

And so, while its entertainment role is gone, the *"third floor"* has again attained an air of respectability where the ghosts of thespians and musicians might add an unseen touch of class to the building.

Two former Arnpriorites who have done well in the acting field locally before moving to Ottawa are, Bernard McManus who participated in many character roles, then went on to direct several Orpheus Society and other Ottawa theatrical productions before performing on television; and F. X. *"Ebbie"* Lavoie, both of whom perfected their histrionic ability under the tuition of Mae Rouselle a former teacher and elocutionist with the Arnprior High School staff.

There have been Little Theatre and Church drama groups who have staged some outstanding performances in latter years and the Arnprior District High School Drama Club has won some prestigious awards in Ontario Drama festivals in recent years under the able direction of Stuart Morrison and Arlene Avdovich both specialists in the art of drama.

THE ORIGINAL VILLAGE HALL

ARNPRIOR'S FIRST Village Hall, a frame constructed building on Victoria Street where the Pentecostal Church is presently located, was destroyed by fire on April 2, 1888. The building was small, not sufficiently large enough to hold public gatherings. Council meetings were held there and the Victoria Fire Company maintained a hose tower adjacent to the Hall.

Immediately following the fire, Village Council set in motion the necessary steps to build a new Hall. A by-law, in June 1888, for authority to issue debentures in the amount of $12,000 for the purpose of erecting a new Hall on the old site was defeated, primarily because it was felt the location was not suitable for the proposed new building. The matter remained deadlocked until McLachlin Brothers offered, free to the town, a parcel of land at the junction of Elgin and Madawaska Streets. The by-law for the same expenditure but with the building on the new site, was reintroduced and approved by the ratepayers in July 1888. Tenders were called and the contract was awarded to Robert Fleming for $11,760. The architect was Andrew Bell of Almonte. The new Hall was completed in the summer of 1889. It is said it would cost $1.5 million to replace the structure today. The Council of the day was: Reeve, R. G. Moles; Councillors, Doctor James G. Cranston, Peter McGonigal, Joseph McDougall and Archibald Campbell. The Village Clerk was George E. Neilson; the Treasurer, John Tierney.

The by-law was as follows: *"By-law No. 228, a by-law to raise by way of loan the sum of Twelve Thousand Dollars, for the purpose therein mentioned,"* Signed by James Bell, Clerk. At the time the existing debt of the Village was $3,992.60 plus interest $1,510.15. The total assessment was $501,163.00. The vote of the electors was held July 30, 1888.

BANDS OF BYGONE YEARS AND PRESENT

THERE WERE not "76 Trombones" in any of the many old-time once popular bands in Arnprior, but there were many more than "76" if one counts all of the "slide trombones" that helped make up the composition of the various bands that played in Arnprior down through the years.

Among the great Bandmasters of other years who helped organize and develop Arnprior bands, were Charles P. Dontigny, member of a renowned Arnprior musical family; Captain Albertson, a retired Canadian Army officer who had conducted military bands prior to coming to Arnprior, and George Gazley.

There is nothing quite like band music and the Arnprior District High School Band, under the direction of Bandmaster Ted Graham, is keeping alive this tradition that played a very prominent role in Arnprior in bygone years. The school band has been conducted by Graham, a member of the teaching faculty, for the past nine years. Its beginning came about a number of years ago when vocal music was being taught by Denis Punter and John McPhail. Band instruments were eventually acquired and the band became a reality. Other band leaders were John Storie and Ulo Valdma, both at one time members of the teaching staff.

The Arnprior Citizen's Band of 1887, under the direction of Charles Dontigny, assumed a rather novel position in the scheme of Christmas and New Year celebrations. A holiday greeting card from the band read: "We will be pleased to serenade you at your residence on the afternoon of New Year's Day, January 1, 1887, under the leadership of Charles P. Dontigny." The card was signed by Terry Brady, Secretary-Treasurer.

Back in 1923, the Arnprior Fire Brigade sponsored a sort of resurrection of the one-time Firemen Marching Bands and among the personnel of that 1923 band were many widely known qualified musicians. Among these was Ernie Wolff. Ernie could extract from a trumpet that melody and rhythm that has made the instrument a favorite with the big-time bands of years ago.

Thomas W. McElligott was an artist with a Snare Drum; Dan O'Connor played the B Flat Clarinet, with the Parsons Brothers George and Gerald, playing Trumpets; James Hart played the Trombone and Harry Jones was an excellent Trumpet player. Also included in the personnel of that 1923 Band were: President, Mayor Thomas Church; Vice-President, Michael Lynn; Bandmaster, George Gazley; Walter Lyon, Bass Drum; A. Bell, E Flat Bass Horn; Carl Wolff, Alto Horn; Ernie Davies, E Flat Clarinet; Emile Woermke, Alto Horn; Findley Macnab, B Flat Clarinet; Bill Wolff, Baritone Horn; Fred Smith, E Flat Bass; and a second Fred Smith played a Trumpet; Les Scheel, Double B Flat Bass; Herman Woermke, Trombone; Jack Kewley, John Lyon, Oswald Lewis, Hugh McGill and Wilfred Slater.

It was in 1916 that Captain Albertson became Band Leader and instructor for the 15 member Firemen Band.

Among those under the tutorage of Albertson was Ernie Wolff who recalls playing on the march on the field where now stands St. Joseph's school. Albertson taught the group the art of playing while marching, even though many of them found it difficult enough to learn to march properly let along play on the march, but they were successful under Albertson in achieving some perfection. The Band eventually became known as the Arnprior Band and they conducted numerous concerts up until the mid-twenties. There was little, if any, financial support for the Band other than the occasional door-to-door canvass and collections at concerts. The instruments originally belonged to the Arnprior Fire Department. Concerts were conducted throughout Valley towns, at Fall Fairs, Strawberry Festivals and important holidays and picnics at McLachlin's Grove.

Interesting is the fact that there were several brother acts in that 1923 Band. The three Wolff brothers, Ernie playing the Trumpet; Carl, the Alto Horn; and Bill, a Baritone Horn. Then there were the Parsons brothers, George and Gerald, both Trumpet players. There were the Woermke brothers, Emile, Alto Horn and Herman, playing the Trombone.

During the summer of 1930 the Kenwood Band was organized. Instruments were supplied by Kenwood. Noted Bandmaster Charles Payette conducted the group for a time. Among the personnel of this band were: Harry Jones, Charles Mulcahy, Edgar Frieday, Earl Bethune and Herb Berndt, all playing Cornets; Ed Bond, Owen Herrick, Alex Staye, Albert Lamorie and Wilfred Chabot, Clarinets; Carl Wolff and Charles Frieday, Alto; Jim Hart and John Legault, Trombone; Frank Whyte, Baritone; Augie Schwab and Harry Buder, Bass; and Edgar "Tid" Dontigny, Drums.

BRANCH No. 174 ROYAL CANADIAN LEGION

IT WAS immediately following the First Great War that returning members of the Armed Forces, recognizing the need of an organization to act in the interests of veterans and their dependents, formed the Great War Veterans' Association in Arnprior in May 1919, with James Brennan the first President of the fledgling society and Thomas W. McElligott as Secretary-Treasurer. Among others who served on committees were: Frank Kerr, Colonel P. H. Gardner, Noble Armstrong, Hector Frappier, Willard McNeil, John Meek and Lloyd Cartwright. At the close of 1919 the GWVA had a membership of 200. Meetings were first held in the Council Chambers, later in the Galvin Block, then to the Cameron Estate on Madawaska Street. In 1921 Colonel Gardner assumed the office of President and served in that capacity for two years. He was succeeded by Lloyd Cartwright who was President during the final four years of the organization. McElligot served as Secretary-Treasurer during the entire life of the Great War Veterans' Association in Arnprior. Padre of the Branch was Rev. H. W. Cliff who remained in this capacity until the breakup of the group. A Ladies Auxiliary also acted for some years.

Interests in the GWVA were primarily the same as those of the present Canadian Legion. A special fund was set aside at Provincial Command, called the Widow's and Orphans' Fund, with a percentage of annual dues apportioned to this cause.

It was May 28, 1930 that a meeting was set up for the purpose of organizing a branch of the Canadian Legion of the British Empire-Service League in Arnprior. The first executive elected was: President, Percy H. Gardner, Secretary, J. Clarence Irvine; 1st Vice-President, Harold A. Short; 2nd Vice-President, J. E. Steen; Treasurer, A. G. Burwash; Executive Committee, Dr. J. H. Box, Dr. J. L. Sanders, J. H. Melanson, Honorary President, David Craig, a veteran of the Riel Rebellion. Also named to the Executive Committee were: J. A. Ferguson and F. H. Bronskill. Charter members of the Arnprior Branch were David Craig, P. H. Gardner, H. A. Short, J. E. Steen, A. G. Burwash, J. C. Irvine, J. H. Melanson, Dr. J. H. Box, Dr. J. L. Sanders, J. A. Ferguson, F. H. Bronskill, John Q. Meek, MM, DCM, John R. Hill and R. Ruddick. The first Padre was Rev. A. E. McAteer.

Since that beginning the Royal Canadian Legion Branch 174 has reached auspicious heights. They have a beautiful building located on Daniel Street and are considered among the top Canadian Legion service orgnizations in the country. Some of the community activities sponsored by the Branch include: Scholarship Programs, Public Speaking, Veterans' Housing, support for the local hospital, Service Bureau re. Veterans' Affairs Department, Construction of the Cenotaph in 1952, Boy's Band and Cadets, Ladies Auxiliary organized in 1949 and the new Legion Hall completed September 1949 and officially opened for meetings October 16, 1949.

Branch 174 has provided excellent leadership down through the years with some of their members achieving high office, including Ian G. Malloch, Chairman of the Provincial Committee Province of Ontario, who is also a former Zone Commander and District Officer; Paul Bertrand, and William Meek, both former Zone Commanders and District Officers.

The Presidents of the Royal Canadian Legion Branch 174 are as follows:

1930	P. H. Gardner
1931	H. A. Short
1932	R. R. Rose
1933-34	J. C. Irvine
1935	J. R. Hill
1936	Noble Armstrong
1937	J. C. Irvine
1940	S. D. Hall
1942	A. V. Charbonneau
1944	A. J. Hamel
1945	George Chabot
1946	Rev. A. Mills
1947	Ian Malloch
1948	G. Martin
1949	K. W. McNab
1950	M. Blevins
1951-52	T. J. Barton
1953	Ian Malloch
1954-56	W. L. Sinnett
1957-59	Paul Bertrand
1960-61	Kerry Dunphy
1962-64	Ian Malloch
1965	E. Miller
1966-68	W. H. Meek
1969	A. Bond
1970-71	J. Bowman
1972	Al Hahn
1972-73	Ron Watson
1973-75	William Parsons
1975-77	Leo Moskos
1977-79	C. N. Tearle
1979-82	L. P. Summerfield
1983-84	Wayne Gerrie

1938, 1939, 1941 and 1943 missing

ARNPRIOR FIRE DEPARTMENT

IT IS ALMOST 100 years since Arnprior's first volunteer fire department, the Victoria Fire Company, handed an ultimatum to the Arnprior Village Council stating that unless they were paid twelve dollars per year each, for the services of the approximately twent-four man brigade, they would resign in a body on August 1, 1888.

The Fire Committee of Council, however, called their bluff, took immediate action and organized a new company. Over forty volunteers were speedily recruited; a meeting was held organizing the new brigade re-named the Victoria Hook & Ladder Company. An election of officers was held with the following results: Captain, David Craig; 1st Lieutenant, Hiram Johnston; 2nd Lieutenant, B. W. Devine, Fireman, James H. Adams.

Membership in the original Victoria Fire Company included: Captain, J. P. Galvin; 1st Lieutenant, R. B. McCreary; Fireman, James Gadbois; Secretary-Treasurer, Edwin Farmer; No. 1 Reel, John D. Lee; No. 2 Reel, John L. Harvey; Protector of Hose, R. A. Hunt; Coal Cart, John Cunningham; Branchmen, William Davies, Henry Hicks, Napoleon Cousineau, A. Menzies, D. H. Conley, Joseph McDougall, Hiram Johnston, M. D. Graham, W. J. Hammond, William Connors and William Prensler.

But from the very beginning of the first brigade to the present day, members of the volunteer fire fighters have been dedicated and fearless men, battling many catastrophic blazes against terrible odds, particularly in the early years when the village was predominately composed of frame constructed dwellings and business places creating a hazardous situation that might well have made the community vulnerable to devastation by fire. There is a history of involvement that most people just take for granted, yet the Fire Department along with the Police Department, make life safer for everyone.

In the 1890's the Victoria Fire Hook & Ladder Company numbered 27 men and they were a dashing crew attired in natty blue and white parade uniforms at various demonstrations throughout the Valley. The group specialized in fancy drill under the direction of Sergeant Patrick Garrick who had held a commission from the Military College in Hythe, Ireland.

A key man in the organization was William Prensler, caretaker and general *"jack of all trades"* at the Town Hall for some fifty years. When a fire alarm was turned in, Prensler rang the *"fire"* bell tolling out the wards. Then he fired the steam pumper which was horse-drawn to the scene if required. The town was divided into wards. Number 1 at the Town Hall; Number 2 at the Market Place near the corner of Victoria and what is now Bell Streets; Number 3 originally located on William just off John Street then moved to a location on William Street between John and Daniel Streets; Number 4 was on McLachlin Street near the Lutheran Church; Number 5 was McLachlin Brothers lumber yards. McLachlins also had their own fire fighting equipment and this was named the *"Mill Brigade"*.

Hose lines were on reels mounted on two-wheel carts. An eight foot wagon tongue extended from the cart and four to six men would haul the fire fighting apparatus to the blaze. And they did this at a fast run developed over many hours of rehearsal.

The crew manning number 4 hose house included, Captain Eric Baumann, Len Slater, Norman Smith, Bill Gutzman and Jack Staye. They practised evenings. The routine included hurrying to the hose house; then running the reels to the hydrant; ladder practice consisting of two men holding the heavy ladder, two would run up the extension and Gutzman was adept at climbing the ladder with great speed. This Number 4 crew consistently had the best time in Valley competitions between fire fighters from Renfrew, Almonte, Carleton Place and Arnprior.

The first Fire Chief on record was Bob Neill, who operated a blacksmith business which was later owned and operated by Sam Pritchard.

WILLIAM G. "BILL" BEATTIE

CLASSED AS the perennial Fire Chief of Arnprior, Bill Beattie, a slim, strapping, six foot one inch, good looking fellow, was a particularly imposing looking figure when decked out in his Fire Chief regalia. Beattie appeared predestined to the Arnprior Fire Department. When he hopped off the train on his first visit to Arnprior in 1896, a bad fire was in progress and he was pressed into service and in his best clothes. Born in Bryson, Quebec, January 3, 1875, he came to Arnprior to work with McLachlin Brothers. In 1901 he joined the staff of Sanitaris and later was employed with the Brewer's Warehousing Company where he worked for 36 years.

Fire Chief William Beattie

Photo courtesy Muriel Sanders

Beattie became Chief in 1914 and remained head of the department until 1954. On January 12, 1958 he was honored by his fellow firemen and presented with a silver tea service and a cheque by the then Deputy Reeve, later Cabinet Minister and Senator, J. J. *"Joe"* Greene. He died in 1969 at the age of 94. Beattie liked to reminisce on the early days of fire fighting when Arnprior's streets were literally muddy pot holes through which men hauled the reel carts with mud and slush sometimes pouring over the hubs. His pay for his first year with the brigade was $1.75.

Back in 1929 and for many years later, the ringing of the fire alarm bell at the Town Hall meant something to the general public. In addition to the fact that it indicated trouble, the alarm system was divided into wards for fire alarm or disaster purposes somewhat similar to previous years. Following the sounding of the general alarm, the bell would strike the ward effected. One stroke of the bell indicated the fire was in Ward Number 1, the district bounded by the Madawaska River, Madawaska Street to the Town Hall, Elgin to McLachlin Street, thence to the CNR tracks and along the CNR to the Madawaska River. Number 2 Ward was for all that portion of the town north of the district in Number 1 to the Ottawa River.

Number 3 Ward indicated the blaze was in that section of the town south of the CNR tracks and from the Madawaska River west to Edward Street. Number 4 Ward embodied all that section of the town south of the CNR tracks and west of Edward Street. At the conclusion of the fire the bell was struck twice as a recall and to inform householders that the fire had been extinguished. Harry Slaughter, whose home was near the Town Hall, recalls as a young boy, he and his seven brothers racing across Madawaska Street to the hall to learn first-hand, from Bill Prensler, the exact location of the fire. They would often arrive on the scene before the firemen.

Some of the big fires that left an indelible impression on the mind of Chief Beattie were the Shirt Factory, the Campbell House blaze on September 30, 1923 in which one man perished and which created extensive damage along John and Elgin Streets. He also recalled the July 4, 1910 fire at the Gillies Brothers lumber yard when 29 million feet of lumber burned. A yearly Ogdensburg excursion train had to be held in Arnprior because railway ties adjacent to the fire were burning.

HENRY TOURANGEAU

ARNPRIOR'S THIRD Fire Chief, Henry Tourangeau, resided in the Town Hall and, like Bill Prensler, was the man for all seasons around the administrative building, caretaker, turnkey, fire alarm controller, as well as Fire Chief. Henry Tourangeau was a member of the fire department for 35 years until retirement.

CLETUS GREEN

FOLLOWING THE retirement of Henry Tourangeau, Cletus Green, also a long time fireman, became Chief for about one year, after which he was succeeded by former Chief Henry Tourangeau's son Stanley.

STANLEY TOURANGEAU

A "FIRE FIGHTER turned artist", a rather inconceivable combination but that is what Stan Tourangeau was. While he is a fireman no longer, Stan Tourangeau is recognized as one of the country's finest artists. Some of his works are in England, Belgium and Australia, while hundreds hang on walls throughout Canada. Despite some health handicaps, Tourangeau is still turning out lavish paintings, not so much for the money involved but for keeping an active interest in an art he acquired in elementary school where he used to paint flowers and scenery on fruit jars and pieces of glass. A self-taught artist, he learned to paint through reading various books and he plays down the general opinion that painting is indeed a difficult art. When he sits before his easel, brush or pallet knife in hand, Tourangeau begins to relax. He can complete a painting in an evening, sometimes in an hour and a half. When commencing a painting, he sometimes makes a sketch of the subject with charcoal or pencil and quite often will paint from a colored photograph. One of his more beautiful achievements hangs on the wall in the Mayor's office, a painting of the D. A. Gillies building,

the former Post Office, presently the library and museum. More remarkable is the fact that he continues his artistic work despite a cataract on his right eye and the left eye blind.

Photo by Hanson

Fire Chief Stanley Tourangeau

But to get to Stan Tourangeau, the fire fighter. The family lived in the caretaker's quarters at the Town Hall during the time Stan's dad was a fireman and Chief of the volunteer brigade and so the youngster was conditioned to the thrills and headaches of being a fire fighter.

At age 19, without the knowledge of his father, Stan applied as a volunteer fireman and was accepted. Referring to his father's reaction, Stan said *"I guess once he found out he was quite happy."* Stan likes to recall some of the fine older fellows who were members of the brigade when he was a youngster, Phil Green, Bill McNeill, Alex Closs, Bill Abraham and *"Kip"* Cotie — *"all good fellows and good firemen"* said Tourangeau.

Stan Tourangeau joined the fire department in 1936 and retired in 1972 after having served 36 years, 11 of which as Chief. The only break was two years while he served in the RCAF. It was during a western posting that he met his future wife, Claire, at St. Victor, Saskatchewan. There is little doubt that the years of being Chief had taken their toll on his health. Innumerable are the times during his career when he was awakened during the night to fight a blaze, many of which were fought in numbing cold, in ice-caked clothing and ordinary rubber boots often filled with water. Speaking of some of the disastrous fires he fought, Tourangeau recalls the Laderoute fire on Victoria

Street when a mother and baby died as a result of the blaze; the Green Dragon Restaurant fire, one he termed *"hard to fight and nearly costing the lives of three children"*. The Stedman blaze and the Madawaska Hotel were other very bad fires. He recalls a fire in the Gillies lumber yard so severe that firemen had to be watered down by hose in order to get nearer the blazing lumber piles.

Following his retirement Tourangeau was the guest of honor at a Lions Club *"Stan Tourangeau Night"* where he was presented with a plaque and a gift of money. Still maintaining a close affection for his fire fighting comrades, Stan said, *"the Fire Department has never forgotten me"*. Only recently they presented him with a dress uniform. He was also presented with a plaque from the Association of Canadian Fire Chiefs. Tourangeau is also the recipient of Canada's Centennial Medal in recognition of his service. He has good words for the various industries in Arnprior who permit their personnel, who are members of the Fire Department, to leave the job to attend fire duty.

Following Stan Tourangeau's retirement, Orville Bullard served as Chief for a while pending the arrival of Leonard Mills, the town's first full-time Fire Chief. Mills served from 1972 until 1976.

THOMAS BURNETTE

ALONG WITH Stan Tourangeau, Tom Burnette is among the youngest Fire Chiefs in the history of fire fighting in Arnprior. Joining the volunteer brigade in 1965, Burnette became full time Chief in

Fire Chief Thomas Burnette

Photo by Hanson

May, 1976. With his volunteer department consisting of 21 men, he has fought some difficult fires in his day, mentioning the A. F. Campbell & Son blaze, the Gillies Brothers fire of recent years, the Rudd Block and the High School fire.

Tom Burnette, a genial man, is well qualified for the position of Chief. He has attended many instructional courses at the Ontario Fire College at Gravenhurst. Among these was the Fire Protection Technology course, five hundred hours of the study of all phases of fire fighting, a course lasting fifteen weeks. Another course covered the operations of fire protection and fire management. He has also taken a one-week course in arson investigation, also at the Ontario Fire College; and a somewhat similar course at the Ontario Police College in Aylmer. One of the later studies was that of Auto Extrication using the Jaws of Life, which he took at the Ontario Fire College and another such course through Algonquin College. Burnette has also participated in courses of one week duration through the Ontario Fire Marshall's office.

Fire fighting equipment under Burnette's jurisdiction consists of some of the latest fire fighting technological devices including the Jaws of Life, three modern pumper units, an aerial ladder truck, one auxiliary emergency van. These vehicles have all the latest equipment to meet the Fire Underwriters' requirements. All of the firemen are supplied with a radio-paging device, so as to always be available when the need arises. Arnprior is also a member of the Renfrew County Mutual Fire Aid which supplies additional support should this be required. All in all Arnprior has a most efficient and well equipped fire fighting department.

RECREATION

DOCTOR RUSSELL Fraser, in a report on industrial health to the Research Board of Great Britain many years ago, said of recreation, *"Clearly emotional illness is an important cause of industrial disability among employees. The most frequent cause of emotional illness is lack of satisfactory human relationships. Those whose leisure time was spent alone or those with diminished recreational or leisure time interests, suffered a higher degree of emotional illness and had a higher rate of absenteeism than the average."*

The vast majority of people today are in favor of what we now call organized recreation, yet there are those who hark back to the long gone era when everyone created his or her own form of recreation. There are some who believe the child today has lost some of the initiative that was part and parcel of the boy or girl of years ago who had to create their own forms of recreation. This in part, might be so, but when one weighs all the factors along with the advantages of organized recreation as it is today, there is no denying that it helps fill a void that certainly existed in many segments of society in the first half of this century.

It was in 1945 that the Ontario Government amended the Municipal Act and the Ontario Department of Education Act thus enabling Ontario municipalities to appoint an official Recreation Commission and to qualify for grants in aid of municipal recreation. Accordingly, A. A. McLean, Q.C., later Judge McLean, Mayor of Arnprior in 1946-47, set about establishing the necessary Recreation Commission and in this, McLean became known as the father of organized recreation in Arnprior. The first Recreation Director appointed by the Commission was Tom Iveson, a local boy who had served as Recreation Director with the RCAF.

In 1949, Bert Hall, a renowned athlete in his day and now one of Arnprior's most prominent citizens, was appointed Recreation Director and thus commenced an unprecedented career in the field of Recreation in all Canada. It is thought Hall is the only qualified Recreation Director to have remained in one community as Director for a total of thirty years. He retired in 1979, truly Mr. Recreation in Arnprior.

Bert Hall, in addition to a wealth of practical experience in the sporting world, holds an academic degree in Recreation awarded after an intensive three year University conducted course. Further he was awarded the highest statue in the Recreation field in Canada, *"Fellow of the Society of Municipal Recreation Directors of Ontario"*.

Reminiscing on those early years of organized recreation in Arnprior, Hall views his creation of the Senior Citizen Club and the organization of the Minor Hockey League as perhaps the two greatest achievements in a Recreation program that had something for everyone. Recalling the organization meeting of the Senior Citizen group, Hall said there were about 25 people in attendance at the first meeting in the Royal Canadian Legion hall. He picked up Seniors with his own car, chuckling as he mentions one occasion when he called for a lady and drove around the block to pick up another only to have them exclaim that they had not seen each other in ten years. On a picnic to the Robert Simpson Park, he said 75 percent of the Seniors didn't even realize that such a park existed in Arnprior. And when he organized a trip to the National Arts Centre, he found out that some of the Seniors had never been to Ottawa. Church halls and service clubs offered to accommodate the group and entertainment was offered by talented local musicians. The Seniors are presently well organized with their own executive. Meetings and various forms of entertainment are held in the Arnprior Lions Club hall. The Club now boasts a membership of about 300.

The Minor Hockey program initiated by Hall, soared to the point where six hundred youngsters were enrolled in the various groups. Hall devised a system whereby three hockey rinks were created on the single ice surface; this was done by having the rink divided into three cross-wise playing surfaces thus accommodating many more players. In those early years Hall worked 70 hours per week, seven days a week.

The swimming Program in conjunction with the Recreation Commission of the 1960's involved many people of all age groups. Under the direction of Mary Frances Wright, a former Arnprior citizen and an outstanding athlete during her High School days in Arnprior, hundreds received swimming instruction at the local park. Recognized as one of the most highly qualified swimming instructors in Eastern Canada, Miss Wright was a Canadian Red Cross and American Red Cross certified swimming and water safety instructor.

Every phase of recreation was explored and if feasible put into operation. With the cooperation of local schools, among the programs initiated were: dancing classes, childrens' and adult art classes, leathercraft, drafting, blueprint reading, conversational French, public speaking, calisthenics, adult and teenage square dancing, badminton, volleyball, basketball, tumbling, camera club, Little Theatre, shop work, sewing and judo classes.

With the construction of the new Arnprior Curling Club and the new Arnprior District Civic Centre which opened in 1978, the community may well boast one of the finest recreation facilities in the province. The new centre comprises two ice skating surfaces, a 25 meter pool and a community hall, all helping to complete recreational facilities required to provide a full and active urban life style. The new Civic Centre is operated by the Recreation & Community Centres Board which in turn is under the jurisdiction of Arnprior Town Council. The Board is comprised of three members of Town Council and three members at large. The Chairman of the Board must always be a member of Town Council and the present Chairman is William F. Kauffeldt. The Director, Glenn Arthur, is highly qualified to administer the Town's recreation facilities which also include parks and playgrounds. The Recreation staff at the Centre offers active and popular programs for all in the community.

SPORTING WORLD

FOLLOWING THE decline of the lumbering industry, a continuous community development program resulted in a number of industries locating in Arnprior, a transition that has been noteworthy and of tremendous benefit to the Town and its people. Arnprior is serviced by Highways 17 and 29 and is only 60 kilometers from Ottawa; 265 kilometers from Montreal; 425 kilometers from Toronto. The community has access to the St. Lawrence Seaway by short truck or rail connections and both the Canadian National and Canadian Pacific Railways supply service to Arnprior. The South Renfrew Municipal Airport is located adjacent to the town with two paved runways of 2,765 feet. While these physical aspects provide impetus for industrial expansion, recreational facilities have to be a prime consideration when a company is considering locating in a community.

In addition to the recreational infrastructure already mentioned, the town has always been prominent in almost every phase of sports. Some of these are: Cricket, Lacrosse, Baseball, Softball, Hockey, Golf, Curling, Skiing, Bowling, Snowmobiling, Football, Swimming, Sailing, Yacht Club, Skating and Harness Racing. The town is located at the entrance to some of the finest hunting and fishing country in the province and in the Arnprior & District Fish & Game Club, Arnprior boasts one of the most active conservation units in the Province. There are numerous camping grounds in the area amidst a wealth of natural beauty.

CRICKET

In 1863 the first Cricket game ever held in Arnprior was played. Teams from Almonte, Portage du Fort and Arnprior participated. When the game was at its best in Arnprior, some of the players were: Eric Harrington, George Craig, John Campbell, J. H. McLachlin, Dan McLachlin Jr., J. H. Burwash, Joseph McDougall and H. L. Slack. From that beginning the Arnprior Cricket Club began fielding some of the best teams in the Valley.

LACROSSE

Then came Lacrosse and the formation of the *"Prince Arthur Lacrosse Club"*. Among the players of that era were: J. Prudhomme, William Thompson, John Thompson, A. J. Campbell, Claude McLachlin, G. Pearson, J. H. Burwash, Armon Burwash, D. Kiddie, J. McRae, G. Charbonneau, C. Sheppard and R. Belford. The first Lacrosse match the club played against Perth with Arnprior winning. The players wore colorful *"knickerbockers"*. Some of the outstanding lacrosse players of the 1901 era and later were: Pete Thivierge, Charles Laderoute, R. deRenzy, Billy Hayes, Joseph Dupuis, Joe Beattie, Mac Dodds, Jim Murphy, Frank Grace, Albert Dontigny and Jack Dore.

HOCKEY

The 1927-28 Arnprior *"Greenshirt"* hockey team has to be in a class by itself when it comes to hockey history in Arnprior. This was the team that went to the Eastern Canadian Allan Cup playdowns in what was the biggest hockey upset at that point in time. After winning the Upper Ottawa title and eliminating all opposition in the district playdowns, the *"Greenshirts"* went on to meet the high-riding Ottawa Montagnards for the right to represent the Ottawa District in the Allan Cup playdowns. The first game of the two game total goal series was played in Arnprior. This is what happened.

About two minutes after the start of the game it seemed the roof on the old natural ice arena was about to cave in. *"Ebbie"* Goodfellow, a Montagnard star in a team of *"all-stars"*, scored at the 1.40 mark and 25 seconds later Nelson Henry blasted another past Leo Sargent in the *"Greenshirt"* net to make it 2-0. But things began to change; seven minutes later Alex *"Red"* Ferguson led a dash up the ice and pounded the puck past goalie Vic Perrault in the visitor's net. No scoring in the second period but at the 13.15 mark of the final period Dalton *"Dolly"* Olivier, one of the finest hockey players ever developed in Ontario, tied the score and then he came back three minutes later to boom another past Perrault to give Arnprior the win 3-2. Fourteen hundred fans literally blew the place apart.

Special trains were arranged for the return trip to Ottawa on March 2, 1928. Arnprior business places closed down and the old Ottawa Auditorium was packed with 6,500 fans. At 12.05 of the first period, *"Tubby"* Moore put the Monties on equal terms and it remained that way throughout regulation time. The first overtime period was scoreless. *"Tim"* Mulvihill and *"Tick"* Graham took almost simultaneous penalties leaving Arnprior two men short. Archie Dimmell, Olivier and Ferguson held the fort. At 2.30 of the second overtime, Graham fired a *"floater"* from well out. The puck rose high in the air and dropped, trickling into the Ottawa net behind Perrault. The old Auditorium was never to see the like again as hundreds of Arnprior fans poured onto the ice. The Arnprior contingent stopped traffic as they paraded up Bank Street from the O'Connor Street arena, onto Sparks Street and down to the Union Station for the trip home.

The CPR Station in Arnprior was the focal point for those who could not go to Ottawa. When the telegraph operator casually announced, *"Graham scored"*, the place became a bedlam; giant bonfires were started on John Street and the celebrations began. In the Eastern Canada Allan Cup playdowns that followed, the powerful Montreal Victorias defeated the *"Greenshirts"* 5-1 in Montreal and back in Ottawa for the second game won 4-2 to win the series 9-3. There have been scores of fine hockey teams and players in Arnprior down through the years but that 1927-28 team deserves the accolades. Personnel of that team included: Goal, Leo Sargent; Defence, T. C. *"Tim"* Mulvihill and Alex *"Allie"* Ferguson; Centre, Archie *"Pelee"* Dimmell; Right Wing, Dalton *"Dolly"* Olivier; Left Wing, Aldrich *"Ollie"* Mulvihill; Alternates, Harry Slaughter, R. D. *"Tick"* Graham, Harold McGregor, Henry *"Red"* Strike, Sylvester Sargent, Ken Fraser and Bill Daze.

HARNESS RACING

The sport of harness racing in Arnprior evolved from racing on an oval track located on the ice surface of the Madawaska River between the old Elgin Street *"Iron"* bridge and the Canadian National Railway Bridge. The ice racing association was formed by interested horsemen including John R. Byrne, Daniel Byrne, John Brennan and a local veterinarian *"Doc"* Nesbitt. The horses wore specially caulked shoes; sulkies similar to those in modern day harness racing were used, as well as a sulky mounted on steel shod hardwood runners. Harness racing on ice was really the advent of the conventional harness racing as we know it today in this area. The group then organized the Arnprior Driving Club; a tract of land was purchased from Michael Havey and a race track built where the present Agricultural Society grounds are located.

The track is said to be the best half mile track in Ontario. Interest in harness racing increased rapidly; some outstanding horses were developed; purses came into being and with it an entry fee for spectators. The kids were not walking around with a few *"bucks"* in their pockets in those days; they wanted to see the horses run and there was only one way to do it — crawl in under the wire fencing that enclosed the entire north side of the track. Eventually, lumberman John Findley purchased the farm adjacent to the Agricultural Grounds and while he was always interested in horses, this location just added spark to his enthusiasm and he became an ardent horse breeder and harness race driver. It was through his dad that the son, Doctor John S. Findley, gleaned his knowledge and love for horses and racing. After graduating from University the Young "Doc" Findley pursued the business of breeding and racing some of the best horses in the country. His success has been phenomenal. Doctor John is well known in racing circles throughout Canada and the United States. He maintains a stable of horses and operates two training tracks at Arnprior.

ROWING

Various college and other rowing crews on the Thames River in England are prominent and something to see but rowing in Canada is pretty well now confined to an exercise rowing machine set up in a gymnasium or family room in one's residence. But it was not always so. During the first half of the 1900's rowing was the dominant means of travel by water for the average person; the age when rowing was really an art and when it was interesting to watch the different styles used by the rivermen and the pleasure boater of that day.

Despite the fact that he was the owner of one of the finest power boats on the Ottawa River, Tom McElligott Sr. was a pleasure to watch as he manned the oars in a 20 foot square stern "riverman's pointer". McElligott used a leisurely, long stroke that propelled the boat forward at excellent speed. He fixed a mark over the stern, lined it up with a similar point at the bow and seldom turned around to check his bearings.

And another famed old-timer, also a motor boat owner, but one who rowed to and from work at McLachlin's No. 3 sawmill daily, saw-filer Alphonse Vermette, a capable oarsman with an entirely different style. Vermette, used a short snappy stroke with little back bend but he achieved the same results as the rower adopting the longer stroke and back bend. There were scores of row boats on the Madawaska and Ottawa Rivers prior to the outboard motor era.

CONSERVATION CLUBS

Arnprior has always been active in the work of Conservation and Preservation of our natural heritage. Back as far as 1889 there existed the Chats Lake Fish & Game Protection Asociation, an organization that boasted a printed constitution and by-laws booklet, as well as a summary of the Game and Fishery Regulations of the time.

But perhaps the most active and most successful Conservation Club in the history of Arnprior is the Arprior & District Fish & Game Club. It was in the winter of 1947 that a group of some twelve sportsmen from Arnprior and Galetta met in the Galetta Community Club hall to reor-

ganize what was then known as the Lower Mississippi Fish & Game Club, an organization that had been founded in the early 1930's but had become dormant.

The reorganization was successful and because of the greater membership residing within the confines of Arnprior along with more favorable meeting facilities, the club voted to change the name to the Arnprior & District Fish & Game Club. Today the club boasts about 600 senior members plus some 200 in the Junior branch. It is classed among the best Conservation units in Ontario. It owns a clubhouse located in Bell Park at the mouth of the Madawaska River.

ICE BOATING ON CHATS LAKE

In the 1907-1910 era ice boats constructed of wood, something of the appearance of a sleigh with metal runners and hardwood poles extending on each side also equipped with metal runners, were operated on Chats Lake when conditions permitted. The side poles were to prevent the boat from tilting. Proficiency in sailing summer sail boats was a definite asset when one attempted to handle the ice boat. It took a lot of dexterity on the part of the operator and the sport was extremely hazardous in that a strong northwest wind could whip a boat to the open water at the head of the Chats Rapids. The sailing apparatus and sails were similar to that used in the water sailing. The lake had to be well frozen over and free of snow thus cutting down on the number of times the sport could be participated in. Ice boating is said to have had its beginning probably during the era of the Merrick Boat Factory located on Burwash Street.

"WI BESOM AND STANE"

It's a long time since the lads and lassies tossed an iron down the ice on the Madawaska River back in 1865 to get the roaring game a-going in Arnprior.

Nora Ward Wood, Arnprior's Canadian Curling Club Hall of Famer, has compiled a history of curling in Arnprior from the time the first natural ice sheet was built in 1868 on Victoria Street. Other curling rinks were constructed in 1871, 1876, 1899, 1935, 1956 and the present new Curling Club which was built in 1969-70, with four ice surfaces and generous facilities making it one of the finest in the Valley.

The Arnprior Ladies Curling Club was organized on November 20, 1906 with Mrs. H. F. McLachlin elected the first President. Daughter of J. C. Ward one of Arnprior's first curlers, Nora Wood began to learn the art of curling when her father took her to the curling rink when she was eight years of age. She learned the game from experts and in 1954 she was one of the skips to bring the Lady Tweedsmuir trophy to Arnprior for the first time. Although the trophy has been won since by Arnprior ladies the local club is the only Valley organization to have taken the coveted award. In addition to being a former President of the Ladies Curling Club, Wood in 1960, was head of the Royal Caledonia Branch ladies section. She also served as President of the Eastern Ontario Canadian Ladies Association and in 1970 was elected President of the Ontario Ladies Curling Council. Personnel of the victorious 1954 Lady Tweedsmuir rinks were: Mrs. Lorne (Gladys) Rivett, lead; Mrs. Gordon (Peg) Whyte, 2nd; Mrs. A. D. F. (Myrtle) Campbell, 3rd; Mrs. Roy E. (Nora) Wood, skip. Mrs. John R. "Sill" Hill, lead; Mrs. Alex (Jean) Symington, 2nd; Mrs. Walter (Mae) Zadow, 3rd; Betty Olivier, skip. The two rinks were honored with Arnprior Town Crests at a celebration following their homecoming.

In addition to the first Lady Tweedsmuir winners, some of the other excellent lady curlers are: Jessie Lindsay, Alma Fetherston, Mrs. Tom Dore, Mrs. S. E. Johnston, Mrs. J. S. Moir, Goldie Cranston, Mrs. T. S. Church, Gladys Armsden, Mrs. W. A. Whyte, Blanche "Bud" Prensler, Isobel Munro, Vivienne Johnston, Pat McLean and Lori Anderson.

Members of the Men's Curling Club have also brought honor to Arnprior. In 1897 Arnprior curlers won the Quebec Challenge Cup with rinks skipped by W. J. Johnston and Archie Hood. Other members of the winning rinks were J. R. Tierney, James Whyte, R. A. Hunt, Arthur Burwash, Alex Menzies and Hiram Johnston. Arnprior later again won the Quebec Trophy with rinks skipped by Hood and Johnston. Personnel of these were: R. A. Hunt, R. B. McCreary, E. J. Budd, A. C. Pye, A. J. Baker and T. J. Baker.

Again in 1960 Arnprior curlers playing in Cornwall won the Quebec Challenge Trophy, with rinks skipped by Douglas Farmer and A. Steele Campbell. The Farmer rink composed of Walter Flegal, Bernard Laderoute and Doug Macklem, won their game 13-8. The Campbell foursome with Greg O'Neill, Nick Smith and Gerry Neumann, lost 8-6 but the Arnprior rinks took the award with an overall score of 19-14.

Some of Arnprior's best curlers included: Doctor J. E. Murphy, George E. Baker, Charles Baker, Jim Gaudette, W. A. Whyte, E. B. Farmer, Art Farmer, Steve Prensler, J. C. Ward, Roy E. Wood, Allan Beattie, Charles Powell, Douglas Farmer, Lorne Laderoute, Bernard Laderoute, Douglas Macklem, Gordon Whyte, R. M. Simpson, Earl Drysdale, Steele Campbell, Nick Smith, Wilhelm Moe, Allan Ward, Alex Flegal, Blaine Carswell and Harold Lindsay. Another renowned local curler, Bill Burt, was President of the Canadian Branch Royal Caledonia Curling Club.

BASEBALL

There have been many great baseball players and teams in Arnprior. Back in the 1909 era there was the "Pastime" Baseball Club, made up of outstanding athletes including: W. A. Nettleton, Sandy Phillips, Tom Dodd, Joe Simpson, George Valin, Albert Dillabough, Albert Simpson, Joe Murphy, W. J. McNab and William Valin. There was also another team, the "Debators" but little is known of them.

In 1911 there was the colorful Arnprior Colts, with Sid Burwash and Eric Slater forming one of the most potent batteries in organized ball at that time. The Colts wore flashy uniforms, bright red with a white Colt on the shirt. But there was a handicap — the dye had a tendency to run in the uniforms and a player often emerged from a hot, sweaty game, with underwear dyed a startling red. Members of that Colt squad were: Pitcher, Burwash; Catcher, Slater; 1B Dave Caldwell; Shortstop, Harry Dodd; 2B Stan Slater; 3B Fred Schwab; Fielders, Charlie Mulcahy, Bill Armstrong and Bernard "Bunny" Galvin.

Among the great players of the early 1900's was the battery of Jack Dore catching with Aldege Morel pitching. Morel was said to be one of the finest pitchers of the day. Jack Murphy tells a baseball yarn involving Dore and Morel. In those days the umpire stood behind the pitcher. In a game with Carleton Place, the umpire made two calls which Dore questioned; then he made the third; Dore threw off the mask, ran to the pitcher's mound and with one clout knocked six teeth from the umpire and then worried about whether or not he should catch the next train out of town. Then came the league comprising McLachlin Brothers, Kenwood Mills and Cabinet Factory. The McLachlin team boasted an all star battery with E. R. "Dinny" Barnes catching for Ottawa import pitcher Wren Manners. Others with the McLachlin team included Roy Code, Jack Lynch, Ab Bell, Conley and Murphy. Cabinet Factory featured such stars as Evan Farmer, Mac McKenzie, Dinny Galligan and George Marcellus. They were coached by former New Hampshire professional "Gus" Long. The Kenwood Mills team had Augie Schwab, an outstanding catcher and versatile player; Arthur Davieau, Harold Armsden, Harold Short and John Hodecker. Another outstanding pitcher was Clarence Valin. Promoters of the league were Emmett Hogan and Harry Meagher.

Arnprior has had many outstanding softball or fastball teams. New softball diamonds have been completed on Mc-Lean Avenue and it is hoped that sometime in the future a baseball diamond will also be constructed.

SOME NOTED PERSONALITIES

ARNPRIOR HAS had many native sons and daughters who have distinguished themselves in the various professions bringing honor and prestige to the community. While it is not possible to mention all of them, this book recognizes the contribution they have made to the betterment of Arnprior and humanity.

Dr. James G. Cranston, once known by everyone as Dr. "Jim", was among the most highly respected people in Arnprior. Following in the footsteps of his father, also named Dr. James G., who graduated from Queen's University in 1860 and who practiced medicine in Arnprior for many years, young Dr. Cranston attended Queen's as well, graduating in 1895. The younger Cranston joined his father in the medical profession in Arnprior and after the death of his father continued the practice alone in his Madawaska Street residence presently the home of his son Hugh.

During the height of the McLachlin lumbering era, Dr. Cranston was chief medical officer for the company. A sportsman of note, Cranston is mentioned in an article by Frank H. Cooney, one-time resident of Arnprior and later Governor of the State of Montana. In his reminisces Cooney said he watched Jim (Toby) Cranston swim Chats Lake with his brother Percy accompanying Cranston in a row boat. He also mentions *"The Toboggan Boys"* a group which included Cranston, who built a toboggan run at Sandy Hook and later constructed a sail boat which caused apprehension amongst the parents as to their safety. Dr. Cranston died suddenly October 2, 1932 while at camp in the Round Lake area where he had gone for a short holiday with friends from Arnprior. He is the father of Fred, Hugh and Monte Cranston all well-known Arnprior and Valley citizens. Many were the tributes to Dr. Cranston but perhaps the best of all was the poem entitled *"Doctor Jim"* and signed by *"One of the Kids"*. Here it is:

Doctor Jim
I'm freckled and I'm small,
Count for little, if at all,
Dr. Jim

But I have feelin's just the same,
And if I cry, I'm not to blame,
Gee, I feel all limp and lame,
'Cause I'm lonesome for you
Dr. Jim

It's not the same without you,
There was sunshine all 'bout you,
Dr. Jim

I liked to see you smile,
Yet serious all the while,
You frowned on class or style,
Gosh, it's lonesome here without you,
Dr. Jim

I sometimes sit and ponder,
I dream and guess and wonder,
Dr. Jim

Just why it had to be,
That God took you instead of me,
That's sometin' I can't see
'Cept he needed you,
Dr. Jim

Countin' Ma and Dad we number seven,
We all pray to you in heaven,
Dr. Jim

We're certain sure you're there,
You're good enough for anywhere,
Always just and kind and fair,
P'raps the angels will be jealous,
Dr. Jim.

(Signed) "One of the Kids"

Judge Edward J. Houston, born in Arnprior, member of a widely known and highly respected family, was educated in local schools, was a fine athlete and a tremendous credit to the Houston family and his home town of Arnprior.

* * *

J. J. *"Joe"* Greene, former Cabinet Minister in the Trudeau government, later appointed to the Senate. After his call to the Bar, Joe Greene practiced law in Arnprior, married an Arnprior girl, Corinne Bedore, and was a member of Town Council for many years prior to his being elected as Liberal member for Renfrew South. While not born in Arnprior, Joe Greene literally adopted the town as his home and Arnprior adopted him.

* * *

Judge Allan A. McLean, very popular long-time resident of Arnprior, Allan McLean has practiced the legal profession in Arnprior for many years and has served the town well in various capacities including that of Mayor. Judge McLean is known in Arnprior as the Father of Organized Recreation because it was during his term as chief magistrate that he initiated procedure culminating in bringing organized recreation to Arnprior.

* * *

J. W. C. *"Cloud"* Tierney was a member of a pioneer Arnprior family who assisted in the development of Arnprior through their involvement in business and local politics. *"Cloud"* Tierney, a quiet man, was noted for his thoughtfulness and caring for the *"little guy"*. Active in the business world he was a member of Arnprior Town Council for some time and found time for various community and church organizations. Tierney achieved prominence during World War II when he was appointed Comptroller of the Knights of Columbus Army Huts, a position which entailed administration and supervision of the entire project throughout the European and North African theatres of war.

* * *

Judge J. E. Thompson; not too many will remember Judge Thompson who practiced law in Arnprior many years ago, prior to his moving to Whitby following his appointment as Judge. Eleanor Reid Burwash and Catherine Reid Smith, both of Arnprior, are nieces of Judge Thompson.

* * *

Judge Trevor H. Grout; a once prominent figure in legal circles in Arnprior and the Valley. Grout, after being appointed Judge, moved to Belleville.

SERVICE AND FRATERNAL ORGANIZATIONS

ARNPRIOR IS well served by several Service Clubs and Fraternal Organizations. Among these are the Arnprior Lions Club with their affiliates. Fraternal societies include the Knights of Columbus, the Masonic Order and the Independent Order of Oddfellows together with affiliated groups in all three organizations.

The Arnprior Senior Citizen Club is one of the most active Senior organizations in the Valley with approximately 300 members.

The St. John Ambulance organization is most prominent in Arnprior and their humanitarian work is a very definite asset to the community.

FEDERAL STUDY CENTRE

THE TOWN of Arnprior became known, almost on a worldwide scale, during World War II. About 1941 the Canadian government purchased a tract of land on the outskirts of Arnprior and in a few short months an airfield was built; a self-sustaining establishment was constructed on the adjacent land; and the Royal Canadian Air Force commenced the training of hundreds of airmen who were later to play an important role in the War.

The first establishment was known as Number 3 Flying Instructors' School. Airmen from all parts of the British Commonwealth were trained as pilots at the school and upon graduation were posted to duties throughout the theatre of War. The School was later converted to a Flight Engineer Training Centre.

Following the cessation of hostilities the unit was taken over by the National Research Council and still later the Royal Canadian Army Pay Corps operated from the site for a while.

It was in the Autumn of 1953 that the Canadian Civil Defence College was transferred from the Connaught Rifle Range to the former Air Force station at Arnprior. A complete renovation was begun and on February 1, 1954 the Civil Defence people officially assumed control. The unit has had several name changes since then. It became known as the Canadian Emergency Measures College and is now the Federal Study Centre operated by the Public Works of Canada and Emergency Planning. Since 1954 some one hundred thousand students from Canada, United States and NATO countries in particular, have participated in the various courses conducted at the Centre. At the present time, R. Hugh C. Gamble is the Director of Training and Education for Emergency Planning Canada at the Centre; Kenneth McNab is the Senior Development Officer; and Patrick J. Kelly is the Campus Administrator.

CONCLUSION

IN WRITING this history of Arnprior I have carefully researched numerous facets of the subject in order to make the story factual and as interesting as possible. Much of the content is devoted to the founding industry, McLachlin Brothers Limited, and in all truth McLachlins should be recognized as the people who laid the infrastructure upon which our town has been built.

Indeed, God, when creating His Universe, bestowed many natural Blessings on this our Town of Arnprior.

ACKNOWLEDGEMENTS

My sincere thanks and appreciation to the following, as well as those who may have inadvertently been overlooked but nevertheless assisted in making this history of our Town possible.

Arnprior & District Historical Society
    Janet Clancy, President
    Kay Rogers, Chairperson Grant Structure
        Committee
Arnprior Chronicle
    Fred D. Runge, General Manager,
    Runge Newspapers Inc.
Archives - Ontario
Archives - Public
Arnprior & District Memorial Hospital
    Ron Kedrosky, Administrator
Arnprior Primary Health Care Centre
    Gerald Rogers
Arnprior Town Council
    Mayor Thomas Sullivan
    Town Clerk Gary Buffam
Arnprior Museum Board
    Janet Carmichael, Curator
Belden's Atlas' Ross Cumming
Burwash, Edgar Harrington
Caldwell, Ewan R.
Church Representatives
Cunningham, Jean Macnamara
Fulton, Harvey
Graham, Anne and Jean
Graham, Stewart
Hall, Eric Patterson
Hanson, Thomas, Photography
Industrial Representatives
Lindsay, Myra
McCreary, Dr. R. H.
McLachlin, Mrs. Norman
McNab Heritage & Museum Committee
Moskos, Leo
Muirhead, Arnold G.
Mulvihill, Anne
Price, W. R.
Ross, A. H. D., History Arnprior High School
Runtz, Heather Lang
School Representatives
University Women's Club Renfrew & District
Wolff, Ernest B.

ABOUT
THE AUTHOR

Leo Lavoie was born in Arnprior and received his education at the local Separate and High Schools. Following graduation he studied morse telegraphy and became a telegraph operator. At the age of 20 he was appointed Town Agent for the Canadian Pacific Railway, Telecommunications, Passenger and Steamship Departments. Drawing air travel experience as district representative for a large city travel agency, he founded his own agency in 1962 under the name *"Leo Lavoie Travel Agency"*. Active in local Church, Fraternal and Education organizations, he was a member of the Separate School Board for 29 consecutive years, many of these as Chairman of the Board. He served as Chairman of St. John Chrysostom Pastoral Parish Council for four years. In 1963, under the seal of Pope John XXIII, he was awarded the Papal Honor, Knight of St. Gregory. Lavoie also was a member of Town Council for a short period.

Always interested in journalism, he was for 32 years, on a part time basis, the Arnprior and District reporter and feature writer for the Ottawa Journal. His first book, published in 1982, was *"The Church on the Hill"* a history of St. John Chrysostom Parish 1857-1982.

ARNPRIOR YESTERYEAR

McLachlin Residence, now Sacred Heart Convent.
"The Hill" with beach area. Early Lumbering scene, Grist Mill and Sawmills Nos. 1 and 2.

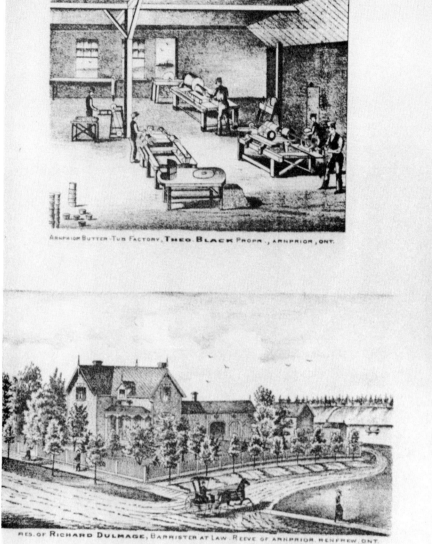

Photo courtesy Beldon Historical Atlas & Ross Cumming. Reproduction by Hanson.

*Butter Tub Factory; The Arcade, now One-Hour Cleaners; Dulmage residence, now Robert Jackson apt. buildings;
Arnprior Marble Works and Quarry.*

Arnprior "Alerts" schoolboy team 1916

Arnprior Fire Department, 1926.

Bank of Nova Scotia, originally Bank of Ottawa, 1874.

Photos pages 100-111 by R. A. Ramsey, Leo Moskos collection, Reproductions by Hanson 1984 ©

James Moskos Confectionery

Old Boy's Reunion, August 1909

J. S. Moir Hardware Building

J. H. McKerracher & Son, Horse Milliners, 1906

ARNPRIOR BAND 1923

Front Row Left to Right: Ab Bell, James Hart, Thomas McElligott, A. Lyon, Mickey Lynn - Vice President, George Gazley, T. S. Church - President, Jack Kewley, William Wolff, Leslie Scheel, Herman Woermke. Second Row Left to Right: Carl Wolff, Emile Woermke, Unkown, Wilfred Slater, George Parsons, Gerald Parsons, Fred Smith, Ernie Wolff. Third Row Left to Right: E. J. Davies, Findley Macnab, Hugh McGill, Walter Lyon, Dan O'Connor, Harry Jones.

John Street 1906

DOMINION DAY PARADE 1914
Mary Lumsden Lewis, daughter Mr. & Mrs. Sam Lumsden, holding reins of pony Teddy; and cousin also Mary Lumsden, daughter of Mr. & Mrs. John Lumsden, Ottawa.

Neil Campbell Block, T. McCormick Grocery

Mansfield Baseball Club

Paving John Street, 1915

Post Office 1906

Canadian Pacific Station and gardens

Photo from bridge

Photo C. Macnamara collection

Whyte Store, Gardner Block. Mrs. J. Lorne Whyte at counter 1908.

Murphy Grocery 1924. Left to right: Mae Savoie Cameron, Annie Murphy and Joe Murphy.

Photo courtesy Mac Cameron

Dagenais Hotel, later Central Hotel and Hotel Madawaska. Jack Mooney behind bar.

Public Archives Canada/C7531/Photo by A. C. McIntyre, photo courtesy E. P. Hall and B. V. Bedore. c 1870.

Grounds and Lumbering Mills

Ontario Archives 52900, courtesy E. P. Hall

Turntable Flat-car, McLachlin Bros.

Photo courtesy Gladys Schlievert

Horseless carriages on John Street, circa 1910.
J. C. "Jiggy" Brennan riding Pig.
Bill Schlievert with his dog team pulling wagon.

Lavoie collection

McLachlin Private School

Photo courtesy K. H. Dunlap

THE LONESOME PINE
*This White Pine Tree was left standing in the middle of Harrington Street for sometime following
construction of Kenwood Mills residences.*

Lavoie collection

Probable type of carriage, transfer Prince of Wales Arnprior-Almonte 1860.

Photo courtesy Jean Macnamara Cunningham. C. Macnamara collection

Grist Mill built by McLachlin

Malloch Sawmill, presently area Old Orchard Estates

Photo courtesy Janet Carmichael

Hiram Robinson in dock

Opeongo trial run, 1909

Alligator Madawaska on Block

Alligator Bonnechere at Arnprior, July 8, 1907.

Roman Catholic Church and first section Separate School.

Logs in Cheneaux Boom 1908

Photo courtesy Ontario Archives. C. Macnamara collection

Scene from south-east bank Madawaska, May 20, 1909.

C. Macnamara collection

McLachlin bush scene, January 1903.

Circus Day, Arnprior 1917

Arnprior Post Office 1904-05, Elgin Street

Edgewood residence

No. 3 Sawmill

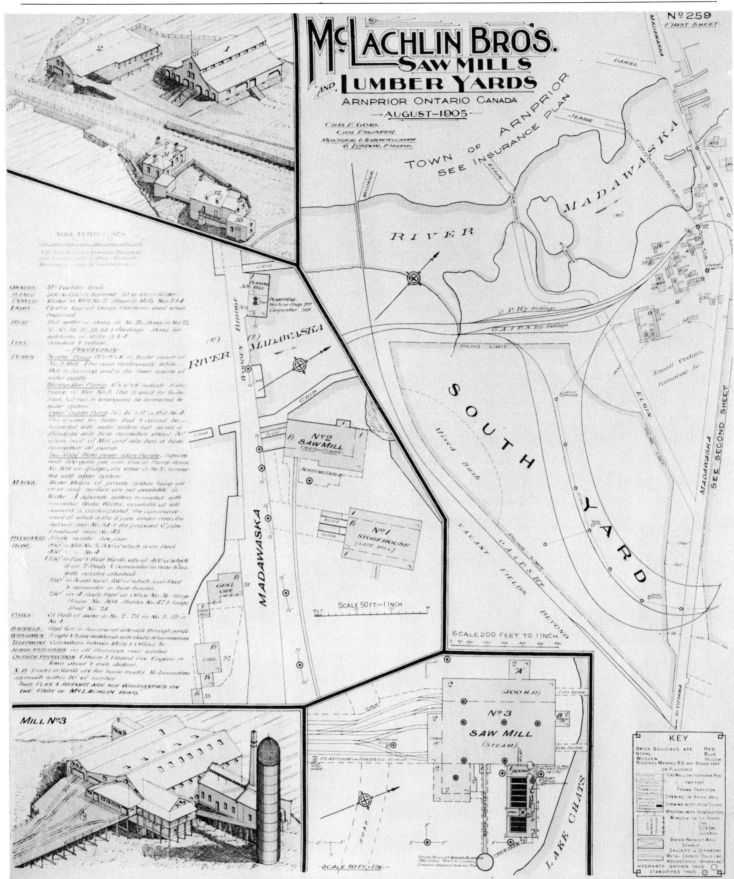

McLachlin Bros. Mills and Yards

Paving John Street 1915

Side-wheeler tug, Donald McDonald

Tug boat Jean Macnamara

Clancy Drug Store and adjacent shops following Campbell House fire 1923.

Hauling wood across Chats Lake

Corner Madawaska and Daniel Streets 1936

Photo courtesy Jean Macnamara Cunningham

Beaver Dam Goodwin's Bay, near Arnprior

Photo courtesy Harry Slaughter

1927-28 ARNPRIOR GREENSHIRT HOCKEY TEAM
U.O.V.H.L., Ottawa and District Intermediate and Senior, Holders Citizen Shield, Beach Trophy, McKinnon Anderson Cup. Back Row Left to Right: Harold McGregor, goal; A. Ferguson, Defence; Dalton Olivier, Right Wing; Harry Slaughter, Left Wing; Kenneth Fraser, Defence; Aldrich "Ollie" Mulvihill, Left Wing. Centre Row Left to Right: William Short, Coach; Leo Sargent, Goal; William Laderoute, President. Front Row Left to Right: R. Graham, Right Wing; Sylvester Sargent, Left Wing; Leo "Buddy" Farrell, Mascot; Timothy C. Mulvihill, Defence; Missing: Archie Dimmell, Centre and Captain; Henry Strike, Right Wing; William Daze, Centre.

Photo courtesy Eileen Hayes

1901 LACROSSE TEAM
Identifiable, Front Row Left to Right: R. deRenzy, William Hayes, Joseph Dagenais, Joseph Beattie, Mac Dodds, James Murphy, Frank Grace. Back Row, second from left, Albert Dontigny.